D0547874

Central Concepts in Biology

Mary Jones and **Jennifer Gregory**

Series editor
Fred Webber

CAMBRIDGE
UNIVERSITY PRESS

PUBLISHED BY THE PRESS SYNDICATE OF THE UNIVERSITY OF CAMBRIDGE
The Pitt Building, Trumpington Street, Cambridge CB2 1RP, United Kingdom

CAMBRIDGE UNIVERSITY PRESS
The Edinburgh Building, Cambridge CB2 2RU, United Kingdom
40 West 20th Street, New York, NY 10011–4211, USA
10 Stamford Road, Oakleigh, Melbourne 3166, Australia

First published 1995
Third printing 1997

Printed in Great Britain at the University Press, Cambridge

A catalogue record for this book is available from the British Library

ISBN 0 521 48501 0 paperback

Designed and produced by Gecko Ltd, Bicester, Oxon

This book is one of a series produced to support
individual modules within the Cambridge Modular
Sciences scheme. Teachers should note that written
examinations will be set on the content of each module as
defined in the syllabus. This book is the authors'
interpretation of the module.

Cover: Manoj Shah/Tony Stone Worldwide

Contents

Introduction

This book is for A and AS level students who have already studied some of the basic elements of an advanced biology course, including cell structure, cell division, the molecular structure of proteins and the behaviour of enzymes.

Two very different subject areas are covered in this book. The first three chapters consider energy transfer within and between living organisms. The last three chapters cover genetic control within an organism, inheritance and evolution. These two areas are both fundamental to a study of biology.

Chapters 1 and 2 deal with the way in which living organisms obtain energy needed to keep them alive. In chapter 1 you will learn how plants transfer sunlight energy into chemical energy in organic compounds, in the reactions of photosynthesis. In chapter 2 you will see how the chemical energy in these organic compounds is released again by the reactions of respiration, usually producing ATP which is then used to provide energy for many different processes in living organisms.

While chapters 1 and 2 look in detail at the biochemistry of these energy-transferring processes, chapter 3 takes a wider view, considering how energy from sunlight is transferred through ecosystems. This chapter also looks at other aspects of ecosystems, describing two important nutrient cycles – those for carbon and nitrogen – and discussing how some human activities can affect the balance within these cycles.

Chapter 4 introduces DNA, explaining how its simple basic structure provides instructions for almost everything that takes place within a living organism. Chapter 5 shows how these instructions are passed on from parent to offspring. Chapter 6 provides a brief description of how natural selection acting on organisms with slightly different versions of DNA codes may lead to changes, or evolution, in the characteristics of the species, and even to the development of a completely new species.

Energy and photosynthesis

1 outline the need for energy in living organisms;

2 describe the universal role of ATP as the energy 'currency' in all living organisms;

3 explain that photosynthesis traps light energy as chemical energy in organic molecules, and that respiration releases this energy in a form which can be used by living organisms;

4 explain the photoactivation of chlorophyll that results in the conversion of light energy into chemical energy of ATP and reduction of NADP;

5 describe in outline the Calvin cycle involving the light-independent fixation of carbon dioxide by combination with a five-carbon compound (RuBP) to yield a three-carbon compound, GP (PGA), and the subsequent conversion of this compound into carbohydrates, amino acids and lipids;

6 describe the structure of a dicotyledonous leaf, a palisade cell and a chloroplast and relate these structures to their roles in photosynthesis;

7 discuss limiting factors in photosynthesis.

The need for energy in living organisms

All living organisms require a continuous supply of energy to stay alive, either from the absorption of light energy or from chemical potential energy. The process of photosynthesis transfers light energy to chemical potential energy and so almost all life on Earth depends on photosynthesis, either directly or indirectly. Photosynthesis supplies living organisms with two essential requirements: an energy supply and usable carbon compounds.

All biological macromolecules, such as carbohydrates, lipids, proteins and nucleic acids, contain carbon. All living organisms therefore need a source of carbon. Organisms which can use an inorganic carbon source in the form of carbon dioxide are called **autotrophs**. Those needing a ready-made organic supply of carbon are **heterotrophs**. (An *organic* molecule is a compound including carbon and hydrogen. The term originally meant a molecule derived from an organism, but now includes all compounds of carbon and hydrogen even if they do not occur naturally.)

Organic molecules can be used by living organisms in two ways. They can serve as 'building bricks' for making other organic molecules that are essential to the organism, and they can represent chemical potential energy which can be released by breaking down the molecules in respiration (page 15). This energy can then be used for all forms of work. Heterotrophs depend on autotrophs for both materials and energy *(figure 1.1)*.

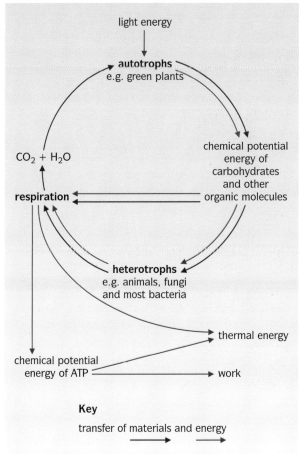

● **Figure 1.1** Transfer of materials and energy in an ecosystem.

Work

Work in a living organism includes:

■ the synthesis of complex substances from simpler ones;
■ the active transport of substances against a diffusion gradient;
■ mechanical work such as muscle contraction and other cellular movements, for example the movement of cilia and flagella, amoeboid movement and the movement of vesicles through cytoplasm;
■ in a few organisms, bioluminescence and electrical discharge.

Energy may also be used to maintain the body temperature. Two of these forms of work, active transport and muscle contraction, will be looked at in more detail later *(boxes 1A and 1B)*.

For a living organism to do work, energy-requiring reactions must be linked to those that yield energy.

In the complete oxidation of glucose ($C_6H_{12}O_6$) in aerobic conditions a large quantity of energy is made available:

$$C_6H_{12}O_6 + 6O_2 \longrightarrow 6CO_2 + 6H_2O + 2870\,kJ$$

Reactions such as this take place in a series of small steps, each releasing a small quantity of the total available energy. Apart from other advantages of multi-step reactions, the cell could not usefully harness the total available energy if all of it were made available at one instant.

Although the complete oxidation of glucose to carbon dioxide and water has a very high energy yield, the reaction does not happen easily. Glucose is actually quite stable, because of the **activation energy** which has to be overcome before any reaction takes place *(figure 1.2)*. In living organisms this is overcome by lowering the activation energy using enzymes and also by raising the energy level of the glucose by phosphorylation (page 15).

Theoretically, the energy released from each step of respiration could be harnessed directly to some form of work in the cell. However a much more flexible system actually occurs in which energy-

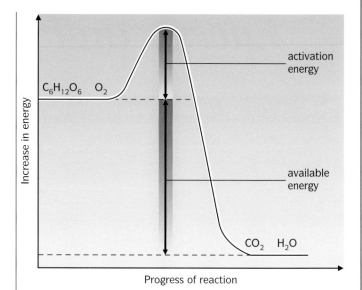

● *Figure 1.2* Oxidation of glucose.

yielding reactions are linked to the production of an intermediary molecule, **ATP** (adenosine triphosphate).

ATP

ATP as energy 'currency'

The structure of adenosine triphosphate (ATP) is shown in *figure 1.3*. It consists of adenine (an organic base) and ribose (a pentose sugar), which together make adenosine (a nucleoside). This is combined with three phosphate groups to make ATP. ATP is therefore a nucleotide (page 41). ATP

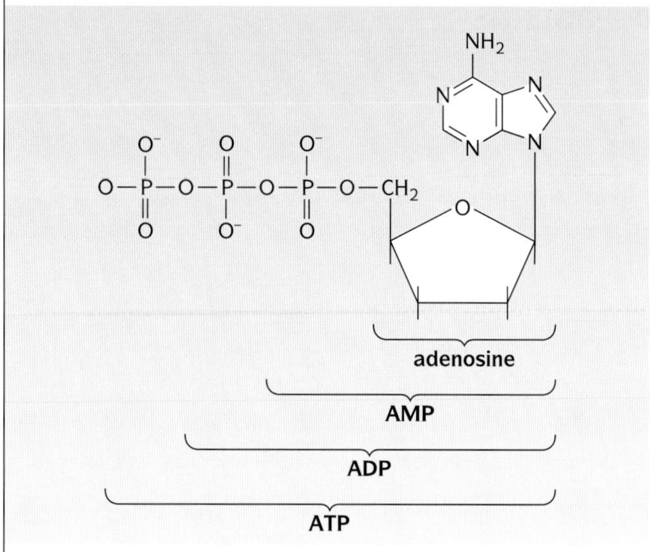

● *Figure 1.3* Structure of ATP.

is a small, water-soluble molecule. This allows it to be easily transported around the cell.

When a phosphate group is removed from ATP, adenosine diphosphate (ADP) is formed and $30.6\,kJ\,mol^{-1}$ of energy is released. Removal of a second phosphate produces adenosine monophosphate (AMP, *figure 4.5*) and $30.6\,kJ\,mol^{-1}$ of energy is again released. Removal of the last phosphate, leaving adenosine, releases only $13.8\,kJ\,mol^{-1}$ *(figure 1.4)*. In the past, the bonds attaching the two outer phosphate groups have been called 'high energy bonds', because more energy is released when they are broken than when the last phosphate is removed. This is misleading and should be avoided since the energy does not come simply from breaking those bonds, but rather from changes in chemical potential energy of all the parts of the system.

These reactions are all reversible and it is the interconversion of ATP and ADP that is all-important in providing energy for the cell:

$$ATP + H_2O \rightleftharpoons ADP + H_3PO_4 \pm 30.6\,kJ$$

The rate of interconversion, or turnover, is enormous. It is estimated that a resting human uses about $40\,kg$ of ATP in $24\,h$, but at any one time contains only about $5\,g$ of ATP. During strenuous exercise, ATP breakdown may be as much as $0.5\,kg$ per minute.

The cell's energy-yielding reactions are linked to ATP synthesis. The ATP is then used by the cell in all forms of work. ATP is the standard intermediary molecule between energy-yielding and energy-requiring reactions. In other words, ATP is the 'energy currency' of the cell. The cell 'trades' in ATP rather than making use of a number of different intermediates.

Energy transfers are inefficient. Some energy is converted to thermal energy whenever energy is transferred. At the different stages in a multi-step reaction, such as respiration, the energy made available may not perfectly correspond with the energy needed to synthesise ATP. Any 'excess' energy is converted to thermal energy. Also, many energy-requiring reactions in the cells use less energy than that released by hydrolysis of ATP to ADP. Again any extra energy will be released as thermal energy (page 24).

Be careful to distinguish between molecules used as energy currency and as energy storage. An energy currency molecule acts as the immediate donor of energy to the cell's energy-requiring reactions. An energy storage molecule is a short-term (glucose or sucrose) or long-term (glycogen or starch) store of chemical potential energy.

Synthesis of ATP

Energy for ATP synthesis can become available in two ways. In respiration, energy released by reorganising chemical bonds (chemical potential energy) during glycolysis and the Krebs cycle (page 17) is used to make some ATP. However, most ATP in cells is generated using electrical potential energy. This energy is stored as a difference in hydrogen ion concentration across some phospholipid membranes in mitochondria and chloroplasts which are essentially impermeable to hydrogen ions. Hydrogen ions are then allowed to flow down their concentration gradient through a protein which spans the phospholipid bilayer. Part of this protein acts as an enzyme which synthesises ATP, and is called ATP synthetase. The transfer of three hydrogen ions allows the production of one ATP molecule. This process occurs in both chloroplasts (page 12) and mitochondria (page 18) and is summarised in *figure 1.5*. The process was first proposed by Peter Mitchell in 1961 and is called **chemiosmosis**.

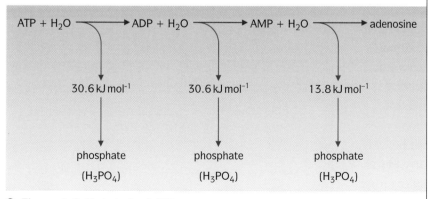

● *Figure 1.4* Hydrolysis of ATP.

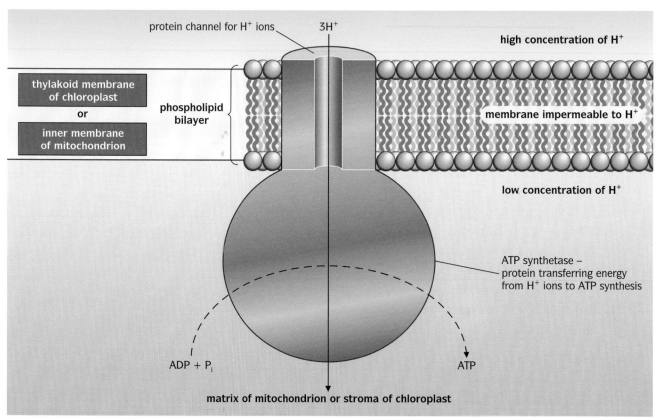

protein channel for H⁺ ions   3H⁺

high concentration of H⁺

thylakoid membrane
of chloroplast

or

inner membrane
of mitochondrion

phospholipid
bilayer

membrane impermeable to H⁺

low concentration of H⁺

ATP synthetase –
protein transferring energy
from H⁺ ions to ATP synthesis

ADP + P$_i$

ATP

matrix of mitochondrion or stroma of chloroplast

● *Figure 1.5* ATP synthesis.

The role of ATP in active transport

Active transport is the movement of molecules or ions across a differentially permeable membrane against a concentration gradient. Energy is needed, in the form of ATP, to counteract the tendency of these particles to move by diffusion down the gradient.

All cells show differences in concentration of ions, in particular sodium and potassium ions, inside the cell with respect to the surrounding solution. Most cells seem to have sodium pumps in the cell surface membrane which pump sodium ions out of the cell. This is usually coupled with the ability to pump potassium ions from the surrounding solution into the cell *(box 1A)*.

The importance of active transport in ion movement into and out of cells should not be underestimated. About 50% of the ATP used by a resting mammal is devoted to maintaining the ionic content of cells.

Box 1A The sodium–potassium pump

The sodium–potassium pump is a protein which spans the cell surface membrane. It has binding sites for sodium ions (Na⁺) and for ATP on the inner side, and for potassium ions (K⁺) on the outer side. The protein acts as an ATPase, and catalyses the hydrolysis of ATP to ADP and inorganic phosphate releasing energy to drive the pump. Changes in the shape of the protein move sodium and potassium ions across the membrane in opposite directions. For each ATP used, two potassium ions move into the cell and three sodium ions move out of the cell. Since only two potassium ions are added to the cell contents for every three sodium ions removed, a potential difference is created across the membrane which is negative inside with respect to outside. Both sodium and potassium ions leak back across the membrane, down their diffusion gradients. However cell surface membranes are much less permeable to sodium ions than potassium ions so this diffusion actually increases the potential difference across the membrane.

This potential difference is most clearly seen as the resting potential of a nerve cell (see *Foundation Biology* in this series). One of the specialisations of a nerve cell is an exaggeration of the potential difference across the cell surface membrane as a result of the activity of the sodium–potassium pump.

Box 1B Muscle contraction

A sarcomere contracts by sliding the thin **actin** filaments over the thick **myosin** filaments. When the muscle is activated by a nerve impulse, calcium ions are released from the **sarcoplasmic reticulum** (specialised endoplasmic reticulum). This allows the myosin heads to bind to the actin filaments. Myosin heads are ATPases and hydrolyse ATP to ADP and P_i which remain bound to the myosin heads. When myosin binds to actin, the shape of the head changes and the ADP and P_i are released. The myosin molecule then changes shape, moving the head with its attached thin actin filament to produce contraction of that part of the muscle cell. This is the 'power stroke'. Then another ATP binds, allowing the actin and myosin to separate. The ATP is hydrolysed and the cycle repeats. Note that the hydrolysis of ATP and the 'power stroke' do not occur at the same time.

When excitation ceases, ATP is again needed to pump calcium ions back into the sarcoplasmic reticulum.

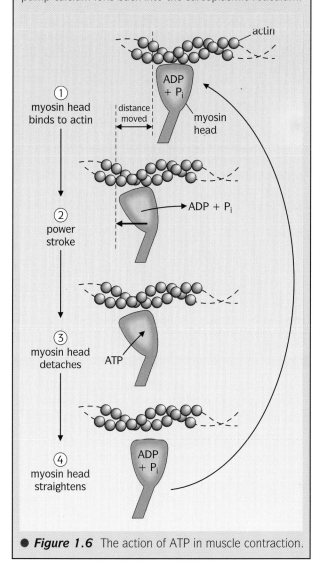

● *Figure 1.6* The action of ATP in muscle contraction.

The role of ATP in the contraction of muscle

The energy for muscle contraction comes from the hydrolysis of ATP to ADP and inorganic phosphate. In resting muscle there is only a small concentration of ATP, and although this supplies the energy which is turned into muscular work, its concentration is about the same in resting and contracting muscle. During contraction the ATP is continually regenerated by a system which involves phosphocreatine (PCr). A resting muscle may contain around $20\,\text{mmol}\,\text{kg}^{-1}$ of PCr compared with $6\,\text{mmol}\,\text{kg}^{-1}$ of ATP.

The ADP produced during muscle contraction is reconverted to ATP by transferring a phosphate group from phosphocreatine, leaving creatine (Cr).

$$ADP + PCr \longrightarrow ATP + Cr$$

However, there is a limited supply of phosphocreatine. It is adequate for a sudden, short sprint lasting a few seconds. After this the phosphocreatine must be replenished via ATP from respiration. If the muscle is very active, the oxygen supply will be insufficient to maintain aerobic respiration in the cells. Then the lactate pathway is used to allow formation of ATP and the muscle cells incur an oxygen debt (see page 20).

Photosynthesis

An outline of the process

Photosynthesis is the trapping (fixation) of carbon dioxide and its subsequent reduction to carbohydrate, using hydrogen from water.

An overall equation for photosynthesis in green plants is:

$$n\text{CO}_2 + n\text{H}_2\text{O} \xrightarrow[\text{in the presence}]{\text{light energy}} (\text{CH}_2\text{O})n + n\text{O}_2$$

carbon dioxide   water   of chlorophyll   carbohydrate   oxygen

Hexose sugars and starch are commonly formed, so the following equation is often used:

$$6\text{CO}_2 + 6\text{H}_2\text{O} \xrightarrow[\text{in the presence}]{\text{light energy}} \text{C}_6\text{H}_{12}\text{O}_6 + 6\text{H}_2\text{O}$$

of chlorophyll   glucose

Two sets of reactions are involved. These are the **light-dependent reactions**, for which light energy is necessary, and the **light-independent reactions**, for which light energy is not needed. The light-dependent reactions only take place in the presence of suitable pigments which absorb certain wavelengths of light. Light energy is necessary for the splitting of water into hydrogen and oxygen; oxygen is a waste product. Light energy is also needed to provide chemical energy (ATP) for the reduction of carbon dioxide to carbohydrate in the light-independent reactions.

Trapping light energy

Light energy is trapped by photosynthetic pigments. Different pigments absorb different wavelengths of light. The photosynthetic pigments of higher plants form two groups: the **chlorophylls** and the **carotenoids** *(table 1.1)*. Chlorophylls absorb mainly in the red and blue-violet regions of the light spectrum. They reflect green light, which is why plants look green. The structure of chlorophyll *a* is shown in *figure 1.7*. The carotenoids absorb mainly in the blue-violet region of the spectrum.

An **absorption spectrum** is a graph of the absorbance of different wavelengths of light by a pigment. The absorption spectra of chlorophyll *a* and *b*, and of the carotenoids can be seen in *figure 1.8a*.

An **action spectrum** is a graph of the rate of photosynthesis at different wavelengths of light *(figure 1.8b)*. This shows the effectiveness of the different wavelengths, which is, of course, related to their absorption and to their energy content. The shorter the wavelength, the greater the energy it contains.

Pigment		Colour
Chlorophylls:	chlorophyll *a*	yellow-green
	chlorophyll *b*	blue-green
Carotenoids:	β carotene	orange
	xanthophyll	yellow

● **Table 1.1** The colours of the commonly occurring photosynthetic pigments

In the process of photosynthesis, the light energy absorbed by the photosynthetic pigments is converted to chemical energy. The absorbed light energy excites electrons in the pigment molecules. If you illuminate a solution of chlorophyll *a* or *b* with ultraviolet light, you will see a red fluorescence. (In the absence of a safe ultraviolet light, you can illuminate the pigment with a standard fluorescent tube.) The ultraviolet light is absorbed and electrons are excited but, in a solution which only contains extracted pigment, the absorbed energy cannot usefully be passed on to do work. The electrons return to their unexcited state and the absorbed energy is transferred to the surroundings as thermal energy and as light at a longer (less energetic) wavelength than that which was

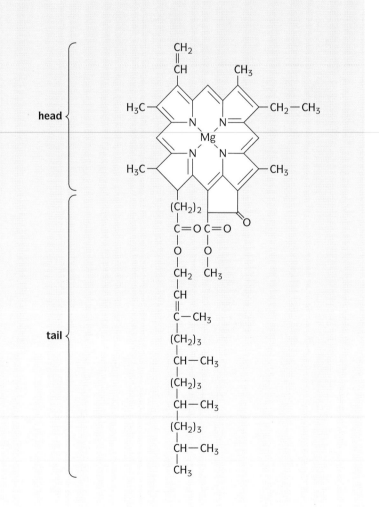

● **Figure 1.7** Structure of chlorophyll *a*.

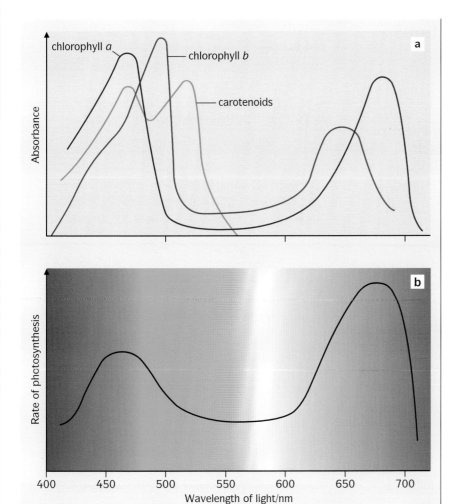

● *Figure 1.8*

a Absorption spectra of chlorophyll *a*, *b* and carotenoid pigments.

b Photosynthetic action spectrum.

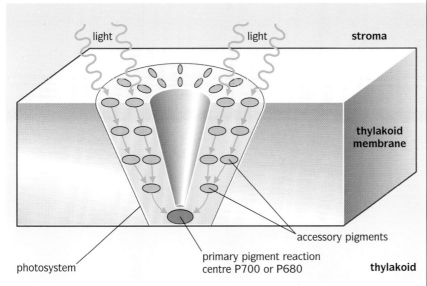

● *Figure 1.9* A photosystem: a light-harvesting cluster of photosynthetic pigments. Only a few of the pigment molecules are shown.

absorbed, and is seen as the red fluorescence. In the functioning photosynthetic system it is this energy that drives the process of photosynthesis.

The photosynthetic pigments fall into two categories: **primary pigments** and **accessory pigments**. The primary pigments are two forms of chlorophyll *a* with slightly different absorption peaks. The accessory pigments include other forms of chlorophyll *a*, chlorophyll *b* and the carotenoids. The pigments are arranged in light-harvesting clusters called **photosystems**. In a photosystem, several hundred accessory pigment molecules surround a primary pigment molecule and the energy of the light absorbed by the different pigments is passed to the primary pigment *(figure 1.9)*. The primary pigments are said to act as **reaction centres**. **Photosystem I** is arranged around a molecule of chlorophyll *a* with a peak absorption at 700 nm. The reaction centre of photosystem I is therefore known as **P700**. **Photosystem II** is based on a molecule of chlorophyll *a* with a peak absorption of 680 nm. The reaction centre of photosystem II is therefore known as **P680**.

SAQ 1.1

Compare the absorption spectra shown in *figure 1.8a* with the action spectrum shown in *figure 1.8b*.

a Identify and explain any similarities in the absorption and action spectra.

b Identify and explain any differences between the absorption and action spectra.

The light-dependent reactions of photosynthesis

These reactions include the synthesis of ATP in **photophosphorylation** and the splitting of water by **photolysis** to give hydrogen ions. The hydrogen ions combine with a carrier molecule **NADP** (nicotinamide adenine dinucleotide phosphate) to make reduced NADP. ATP and reduced NADP are passed from the light-dependent to the light-independent reactions.

Photophosphorylation of ADP to ATP can be **cyclic** or **non-cyclic** depending on the pattern of electron flow in one or both photosystems.

Cyclic photophosphorylation

Cyclic photophosphorylation only involves photosystem I. Light is absorbed by photosystem I and is passed to chlorophyll *a* (P700). An electron in the chlorophyll *a* molecule is excited to a higher energy level and is emitted from the chlorophyll molecule. Instead of falling back into the photosystem and losing its energy as fluorescence, it is captured by an **electron acceptor** and passed back to a chlorophyll *a* (P700) molecule via a chain of **electron carriers**. During this process enough energy is released to synthesise ATP from ADP and an inorganic phosphate group (P_i). The ATP then passes to the light-independent reactions.

Non-cyclic photophosphorylation

Non-cyclic photophosphorylation involves *both* photosystems in the so-called 'Z-scheme' of electron flow *(figure 1.10)*. Light is absorbed by both photosystems and excited electrons are emitted from the primary pigments of both reaction centres (P680 and P700). These electrons are absorbed by electron acceptors and pass along chains of electron carriers leaving the photosystems positively charged. The P700 of photosystem I absorbs electrons from photosystem II. P680 receives replacement electrons from the splitting (photolysis) of water. As in cyclic photophosphorylation, ATP is synthesised as the electrons lose energy whilst passing along the carrier chain.

Box 1C Redox reactions

These are oxidation–reduction reactions and involve the transfer of electrons from an electron donor (reducing agent) to an electron acceptor (oxidising agent). Sometimes hydrogen atoms are transferred, so that dehydrogenation is equivalent to oxidation. Chains of electron carriers involve electrons passing via redox reactions from one carrier to the next. Such chains occur in both chloroplasts and mitochondria. During their passage, electrons fall from higher to lower energy states.

Photolysis of water

Photosystem II includes a water-splitting enzyme which catalyses the breakdown of water:

$$H_2O \rightarrow 2H^+ + 2e^- + \tfrac{1}{2}O_2$$

Oxygen is a waste product of this process. The hydrogen ions combine with electrons from photosystem I and the carrier molecule NADP to give

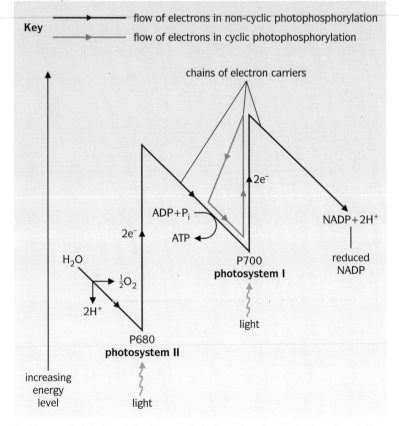

● **Figure 1.10** The 'Z' scheme of electron flow in photophosphorylation.

reduced NADP. This passes to the light independent reactions and is used in the synthesis of carbohydrate.

$$2H^+ + 2e^- + NADP \rightarrow \text{reduced NADP}$$

The photolysis of water can be demonstrated by the Hill reaction.

The Hill reaction

In 1939, Robert Hill showed that isolated chloroplasts had 'reducing power', and liberated oxygen from water in the presence of an oxidising agent. The 'reducing power' was demonstrated by using a redox agent *(box 1C)* which changed colour on reduction. Hill used Fe^{3+} ions as his acceptor, but various redox agents, such as the blue dye DCPIP (dichlorophenolindophenol), can substitute for the plant's NADP in this system. DCPIP becomes colourless when reduced.

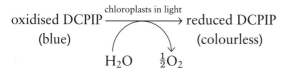

Figure 1.11 shows classroom results of this reaction.

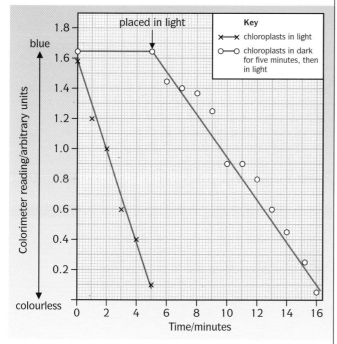

● **Figure 1.11** The Hill reaction. Chloroplasts were extracted from lettuce and placed in buffer with DCPIP. The colorimeter reading is proportional to the amount of DCPIP remaining unreduced.

SAQ 1.2

Examine the two curves shown in *figure 1.11* and explain:

a the downward trend of the two curves;

b the differences between the two curves.

SAQ 1.3

Explain what contribution the discovery of the Hill reaction made to an understanding of the process of photosynthesis.

The light-independent reactions of photosynthesis

The fixation of carbon dioxide is a light-independent process in which carbon dioxide combines with a five-carbon sugar, **ribulose bisphosphate (RuBP)**, to give two molecules of a three-carbon compound, **glycerate 3-phosphate (GP)**. (This compound is also sometimes known as PGA.) GP, in the presence of ATP and reduced NADP from the light stages, is reduced to triose phosphate (three-carbon sugar).

This is the point at which carbohydrate is produced in photosynthesis. Some of these triose phosphates condense to form hexose phosphates, sucrose, starch and cellulose or are used to make amino acids and lipids. Others regenerate RuBP. This cycle of events was worked out by Calvin, Benson and Bassham between 1946 and 1953, and is usually called the **Calvin cycle** *(figure 1.12)*. The enzyme ribulose bisphosphate carboxylase (RuBISCO), which catalyses the combination of carbon dioxide and RuBP, is the most common enzyme in the world.

Leaf structure and function

The leaf is the main photosynthetic organ in dicotyledons. It has a broad, thin **lamina**, a **midrib** and a network of **veins**. It may also have a leaf stalk (**petiole**). *Figure 1.13* is a photomicrograph of a section of a typical leaf from a mesophyte, that is a plant adapted for 'middling' terrestrial conditions (it is not adapted for living in water nor for withstanding excessive drought).

To perform its function the leaf must:

■ contain chlorophyll and other photosynthetic pigments arranged in such a way that they can absorb light;
■ absorb carbon dioxide and dispose of the waste product oxygen;
■ have a water supply and be able to export manufactured carbo-hydrate to the rest of the plant.

The large surface area of the lamina makes it easier to absorb light, and its thinness minimises the diffusion pathway for gaseous exchange. The arrangement of leaves on the plant (the leaf mosaic) helps the plant to absorb as much light as possible.

The upper **epidermis** is made of thin, flat, transparent cells which allow light through to the cells of the **mesophyll** below, where photosynthesis takes place. A waxy transparent **cuticle**, which is secreted by the epidermal cells, provides a watertight layer. The cuticle and epidermis together form a protective layer.

The structure of the lower epidermis is similar to that of the upper, except that most meso-phytes have many **stomata** in the lower epidermis. (Some have a few stomata in the upper epidermis also.) Stomata are pores in the epidermis through which diffusion of gases occurs. Each stoma is bounded by two sausage-shaped **guard cells** *(figure 1.14)*. Changes in the turgidity of these guard cells cause them to change shape so that they open and close the pore. When the guard cells gain water,

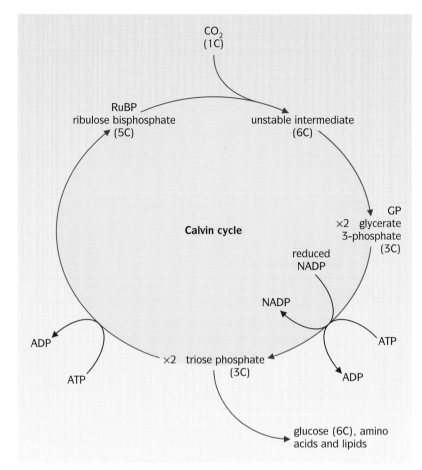

● *Figure 1.12* The Calvin cycle.

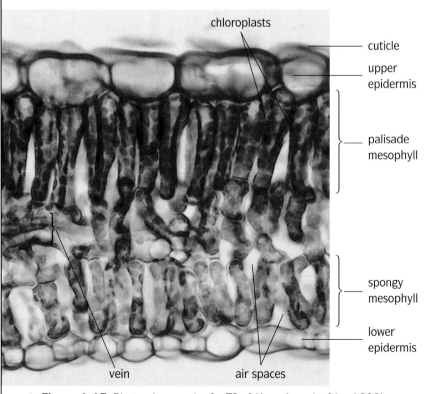

● *Figure 1.13* Photomicrograph of a TS of *Hypericum* leaf ($\times$ 1600).

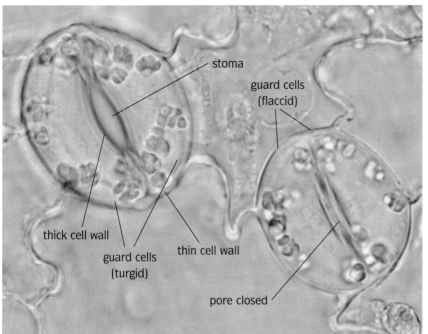

● *Figure 1.14* Photomicrograph of stomata and guard cells in *Tradescantia* leaf epidermis (× 5000).

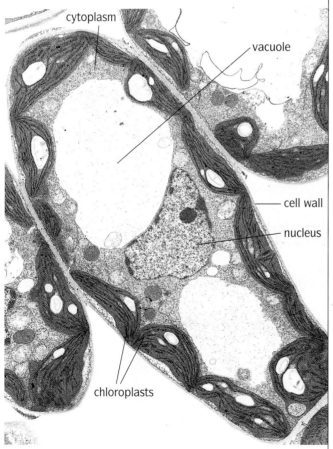

● *Figure 1.15* Transmission electron micrograph (TEM) of a palisade cell from soya bean leaf (× 6000).

the pore opens; as they lose water it closes. Guard cells have unevenly thickened cell walls. The wall adjacent to the pore is very thick, whilst the wall furthest from the pore is thin. Bundles of cellulose microfibrils are arranged as hoops around the cells so that, as the cell becomes turgid, these hoops ensure that the cell mostly increases in length and not diameter. Since the ends of the two guard cells are joined and the thin outer wall bends more readily than the thick inner one, the guard cells become curved. This makes the pore between the cells open.

Guard cells gain and lose water by osmosis. A decrease in water potential is needed before water can enter the cells by osmosis. This decrease is achieved by the active uptake of potassium ions into the guard cells, using energy from ATP.

The structure of a **palisade cell** is shown in *figure 1.15*. The palisade mesophyll is the main site of photosynthesis, as there are more chloroplasts per cell than in the spongy mesophyll. The cells show several adaptations for light absorption.

■ They are long cylinders arranged at right-angles to the upper epidermis. This reduces the number of light-absorbing cross walls in the upper part of the leaf so that as much light as possible can reach the chloroplasts.
■ The cells have a large vacuole with a thin peripheral layer of cytoplasm. This restricts the chloroplasts to a layer near the outside of the cell where light can reach them most easily.
■ The chloroplasts can be moved (by proteins in the cytoplasm – they cannot move themselves) within the cells, to absorb the most light or to protect the chloroplasts from excessive light intensities.

The palisade cells also show adaptations for gaseous exchange.

■ The cylindrical cells pack together with long, narrow air spaces between them. This gives a large surface area of contact between cell and air.

■ The cell walls are thin, so that gases can diffuse through them more easily.

Spongy mesophyll is mainly adapted as a surface for the exchange of carbon dioxide and oxygen. The cells contain chloroplasts, but in smaller numbers than in palisade cells. Photosynthesis occurs in the spongy mesophyll only at high light intensities. The irregular packing of the cells and the large air spaces thus produced provide a large surface area of moist cell wall for gaseous exchange.

The veins in the leaf help to support the large surface area of the leaf. They contain xylem, which brings in the water necessary for photosynthesis and for cell turgor, and phloem, which takes the products of photosynthesis to other parts of the plant.

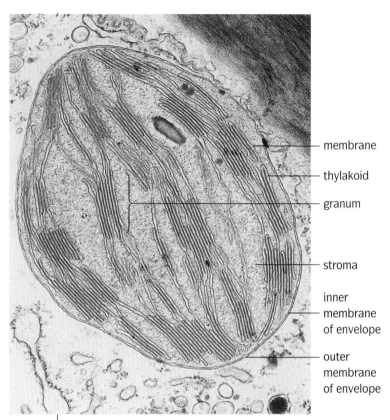

● *Figure 1.16* TEM of a chloroplast from *Potamogeton* leaf (× 27000)

Labels on figure:
- membrane
- thylakoid
- granum
- stroma
- inner membrane of envelope
- outer membrane of envelope

Chloroplast structure and function

In eukaryotic organisms, the photosynthetic organelle is the chloroplast. In dicotyledons, chloroplasts can be seen with a light microscope and appear as biconvex discs about 3–10 μm in diameter. There may be only a few chloroplasts in a cell or as many as 100 in some palisade mesophyll cells.

The structure of a chloroplast is shown in *figure 1.16*. Each chloroplast is surrounded by an **envelope** of two phospholipid membranes. A system of membranes also runs through the ground substance, or **stroma**. The membrane system is the site of the light-dependent reactions of photosynthesis. It consists of a series of flattened fluid-filled sacs, or **thylakoids**, which in places form stacks, called **grana**, that are joined to one another by membranes. The membranes of the grana provide a large surface area which holds the pigments, enzymes and electron carriers needed for the light-dependent reactions. They make it possible for a large number of pigment molecules to be arranged

so that they can absorb as much light as necessary. The pigment molecules are also arranged in particular light-harvesting clusters for efficient light absorption. In each photosystem the different pigments are arranged in the thylakoid in funnel-like structures (*figure 1.9*). Each pigment passes energy to the next member of the cluster, finally 'feeding' it to the chlorophyll *a* reaction centre (either P700 or P680). The membranes of the grana hold ATP synthetase and are the site of ATP synthesis by chemiosmosis (page 3).

The stroma is the site of the light-independent reactions. It contains the enzymes of the Calvin cycle, sugars and organic acids. It bathes the membranes of the grana and so can receive the products of the light-dependent reactions. Also within the stroma are small ribosomes, a loop of DNA, lipid droplets and starch grains. The loop of DNA codes for some of the chloroplast proteins, which are made by the chloroplast's ribosomes. However, other chloroplast proteins are coded for by the nuclear DNA.

Factors necessary for photosynthesis

You can see from the equation on page 5 that certain factors are necessary for photosynthesis to occur, namely the presence of a suitable photo-synthetic pigment, a supply of carbon dioxide, water and light energy.

Factors affecting the rate of photosynthesis

The main external factors affecting the rate of photosynthesis are light intensity, tempera-ture and carbon dioxide concentration.

In the 1900s F. F. Blackman investigated the effects of light intensity and tempera-ture on the rate of photosynthesis. At constant temperature, the rate of photo-synthesis varies with the light intensity, initially increasing as the light intensity increases *(figure 1.17)*. However, at higher light intensities this relationship no longer holds and the rate of photosynthesis reaches a plateau.

The effect on the rate of photosynthesis of varying the temperature at constant light intensity can be seen in *figure 1.18*. At high light intensity the rate of photosynthesis increases as the temperature is increased over a limited range. At low light intensity, increasing the temperature has little effect on the rate of photosynthesis.

These two experiments illustrate two important points. From other research we know that photochemical reactions are not generally affected by temperature. However these experiments clearly show that temperature affects the rate of photo-synthesis, so there must be two sets of reactions in the full process of photosyn-thesis. These are a light-dependent photo-chemical stage and a light-independent, temperature-dependent stage. Secondly, Blackman's experiments illustrate the concept of 'limiting factors'.

Limiting factors

The rate of any process which depends on a series of reactions is limited by the slowest reaction in the series. In biochemistry, if a process is affected by more than one factor, the rate will be limited by the factor which is nearest its lowest value.

Look again at *figure 1.17*. At low light intensi-ties, the limiting factor governing the rate of photosynthesis is the light intensity; as the intensity increases so does the rate. But at high light intensi-ties one or more other factors must be limiting, such as temperature or carbon dioxide supply.

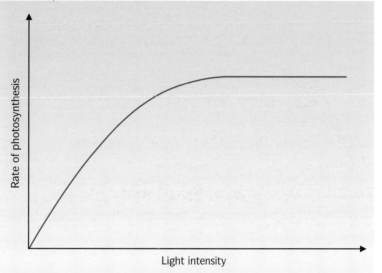

● *Figure 1.17* The rate of photosynthesis at different light intensities.

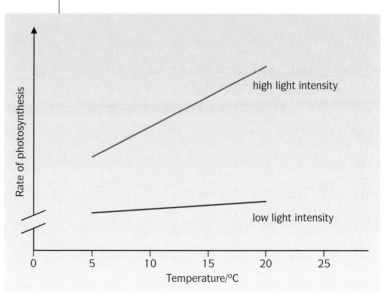

● *Figure 1.18* The rate of photosynthesis at different temperatures.

SAQ 1.4

Examine *figure 1.19* which shows the effect of various factors on the rate of photosynthesis and explain the differences in the results of:

a experiments 1 and 2.

b experiments 1 and 3.

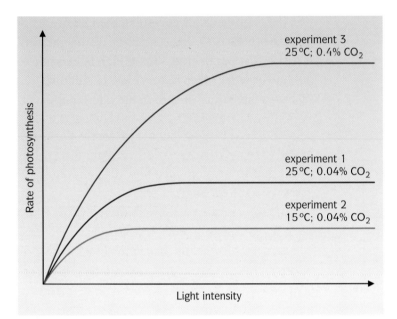

● **Figure 1.19** The rate of photosynthesis at different temperatures and different carbon dioxide concentrations.

Questions

1 Describe the structure of ATP and explain its role as an energy currency.

2 Describe how energy-yielding and energy-requiring reactions are linked in living cells.

3 Discuss the role of pigments and carrier molecules in the light-dependent stage of photosynthesis.

4 Describe the fixation of carbon dioxide in the light-independent stage of photosynthesis.

5 Explain how **a** light energy from the Sun, and **b** carbon dioxide from the air, pass to and are used by the chloroplast during photosynthesis.

6 Give an account of the structure, function and distribution of chloroplasts in leaves.

7 Describe how the light energy of the Sun is converted to chemical energy in green plants.

8 Explain what is meant by the term *limiting factor*. Illustrate your answer by reference to the effects of temperature on photosynthesis.

SUMMARY

■ Organisms must do work to stay alive. The energy input necessary for this work is either light, for photosynthesis, or the chemical potential energy of organic molecules. Photosynthesis traps light energy as chemical bond energy which can later be released and used by cells.

■ Reactions which release energy must be harnessed to energy-requiring reactions. This 'harnessing' involves an intermediary molecule, ATP. This can be synthesised from ADP and phosphate using energy, and hydrolysed to ADP and phosphate to release energy. ATP therefore acts as an energy currency.

■ In photosynthesis, ATP is synthesised in the light-dependent reactions of cyclic and non-cyclic photophosphorylation. During these reactions the photosynthetic pigments of the chloroplast absorb light energy and give out excited electrons. Energy from the electrons is used to synthesise ATP.

■ Water is split by photolysis to give hydrogen ions, electrons and oxygen. The hydrogen ions and electrons are used to reduce NADP and the oxygen is given off as a waste product. ATP and reduced NADP are the two main products of the light-dependent reactions of photosynthesis and pass to the light-independent reactions.

■ Carbon dioxide is trapped and reduced to carbohydrate in the light-independent reactions of photosynthesis, using ATP and reduced NADP from the light-dependent reactions. This fixation of carbon dioxide requires an acceptor molecule, ribulose bisphosphate, and involves the Calvin cycle.

■ Chloroplasts, mesophyll cells and whole leaves are all adapted for the process of photosynthesis.

■ The rate of photosynthesis is subject to various limiting factors.

Chapter two

Respiration

By the end of this chapter you should be able to:

1 outline glycolysis as the phosphorylation of glucose and the subsequent splitting of hexose phosphate (6C) into two triose phosphate molecules which are then further oxidised with a small yield of ATP and reduced NAD;

2 explain that, when oxygen is available, pyruvate is decarboxylated and dehydrogenated, and the remaining two-carbon unit added to coenzyme A to give acetyl (2C) coenzyme A;

3 explain that acetylcoenzyme A combines with oxalo-acetate (4C) to form citrate (6C);

4 outline the Krebs cycle, explaining that citrate is reconverted to oxaloacetate in a series of small steps;

5 explain that these processes involve decarboxylation and dehydrogenation, and describe the role of NAD;

6 describe oxidative phosphorylation, including the role of oxygen;

7 describe the sites of the Krebs cycle and oxidative phosphorylation in a mitochondrion;

8 explain the small yield of ATP from anaerobic respiration and the formation of ethanol in yeast and lactate in mammals.

The glycolytic pathway

Glycolysis is the splitting, or *lysis* of glucose. It is a multi-step process in which a glucose molecule with six carbon atoms is eventually split into two molecules of pyruvate, each with three carbon atoms. Energy from ATP is needed in the first steps, but energy is also released in later steps when it can be used to make ATP. There is a net gain of two ATP molecules per molecule of glucose broken down. Glycolysis takes place in the cyto-plasm of a cell. A simplified flow diagram of the pathway is shown in *figure 2.2*.

In the first stage, **phosphorylation**, glucose is phosphorylated using ATP. Glucose is energy-rich, but does not react easily. To tap the bond energy of glucose, energy must first be used to make reaction easier *(figure 1.2)*. Two ATP molecules are used for each molecule of glucose to make hexose bisphosphate which breaks down to produce two molecules of triose phosphate.

Hydrogen is then removed from triose phos-phate and transferred to the carrier molecule NAD (nicotinamide adenine dinucleotide). Two

Respiration is a process in which organic molecules act as a fuel. These are broken down in a series of stages to release chemical potential energy which is used to synthesise ATP. The main fuel for most cells is carbohydrate, usually glucose. Many cells can only use glucose as their respiratory substrate, but others break down fatty acids, glycerol and amino acids in respiration.

Glucose breakdown can be divided into four stages: **glycolysis**, the **link reaction**, the **Krebs cycle** and **oxidative phosphorylation** *(figure 2.1)*.

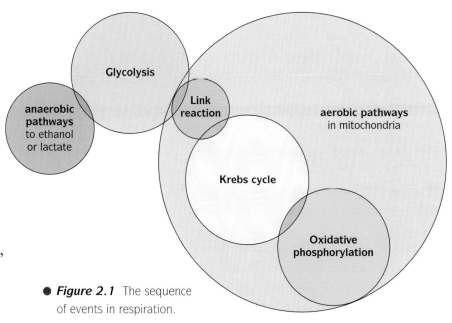

● *Figure 2.1* The sequence of events in respiration.

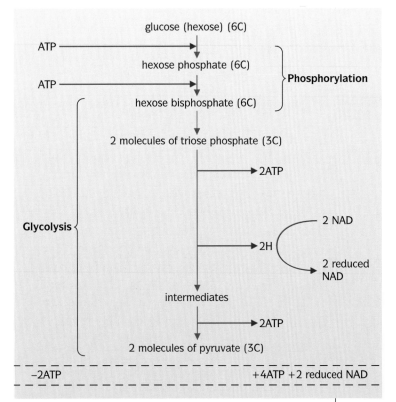

- **Figure 2.2** The glycolysis pathway.

molecules of reduced NAD are produced for each molecule of glucose entering glycolysis. The hydrogens carried by reduced NAD can easily be transferred to other molecules and are used in oxidative phosphorylation to generate ATP (page 17). The end-product of glycolysis, pyruvate, still contains a great deal of chemical potential energy. When free oxygen is available, some of this energy can be released via the Krebs cycle and oxidative phosphorylation. However, first it enters the link reaction.

The link reaction

When pyruvate enters a mitochondrion, it is decarboxylated (that is carbon dioxide is removed), dehydrogenated and combined with coenzyme A (coA) to give acetylcoenzyme A. This is known as the link reaction. Coenzyme A is a complex molecule of a nucleotide (adenine + ribose) with a vitamin (pantothenic acid), and acts as a carrier of acetyl groups to the Krebs cycle. The hydrogen removed from pyruvate is transferred to NAD.

$$\text{pyruvate} + \text{coA} + \text{NAD} \rightleftharpoons$$
$$\text{acetylcoA} + CO_2 + \text{reduced NAD}$$

Fatty acids from fat metabolism may also be used to produce acetylcoenzyme A. Fatty acids are broken down in the mitochondrion in a cycle of reactions in which each turn of the cycle shortens the fatty acid chain by a two-carbon acetyl unit. Each of these can react with coenzyme A to produce acetylcoenzyme A which, like that produced from pyruvate, now enters the Krebs cycle.

The Krebs cycle

The Krebs cycle (also known as the citric acid cycle or tricarboxylic acid cycle) was discovered in 1937 by Hans Krebs. It is shown in *figure 2.3*.

The Krebs cycle is a closed pathway of enzyme-controlled reactions:

- acetylcoenzyme A combines with a four-carbon compound (oxaloacetate) to form a six-carbon compound (citrate);
- the citrate is decarboxylated and dehydrogenated in a series of steps, to yield carbon dioxide, which is given off as a waste gas, and hydrogens which are accepted by the carriers NAD and FAD (flavin adenine dinucleotide);
- oxaloacetate is regenerated to combine with another acetylcoenzyme A. For each turn of the cycle two carbon dioxide molecules are produced, one FAD and three NAD molecules are reduced, and one ATP molecule is generated via an intermediate compound.

The most important contribution of the Krebs cycle to the cell's energetics is the release of hydrogens which can be used in oxidative phosphorylation to provide energy to make ATP.

Although part of aerobic respiration, the reactions of the Krebs cycle make no use of molecular oxygen. However, oxygen is necessary for the final stage which is called oxidative phosphorylation.

SAQ 2.1 _____

Explain how the events of the Krebs cycle can be cyclical.
_____

Respiration

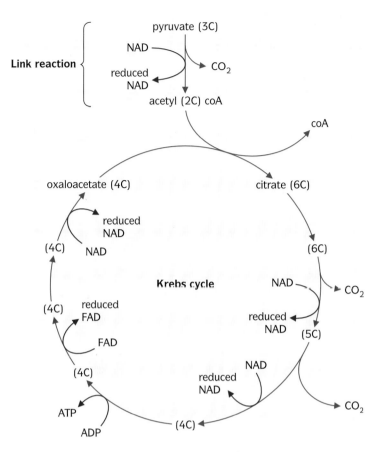

● *Figure 2.3* The link reaction and the Krebs cycle. One turn of the Krebs cycle yields two CO_2, three reduced NAD, one reduced FAD and one ATP molecule.

Oxidative phosphorylation and the electron transport chain

In the final stage of aerobic respiration, the energy for the phosphorylation of ADP to ATP comes from the activity of the electron transport chain. Reduced NAD and reduced FAD are passed to the electron transport chain. Here, hydrogens are removed from the two carriers and each split into its constituent hydrogen ion (H⁺) and electron. The electron is transferred to the first of a series of electron carriers, whilst the hydrogen ion remains in solution in the mitochondrion. Once the electron is transferred to oxygen, a hydrogen ion will be drawn from solution to reduce the oxygen to water (*figure 2.4*).

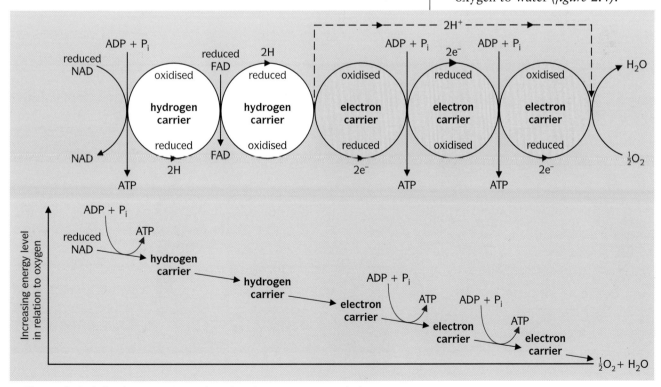

● *Figure 2.4* Oxidative phosphorylation: the electron transport chain.

The transfer of electrons along the series of electron carriers makes energy available which is used to convert ADP + P_i to ATP. As an electron passes from a carrier at a higher energy level to one that is lower, energy is released. This is usually lost as heat, but at particular points in the chain the energy released is sufficient to produce ATP. Three molecules of ATP are produced from each reduced NAD molecule entering the chain, and two ATP from each reduced FAD molecule.

The most widely accepted explanation for the synthesis of ATP in oxidative phosphorylation is that of chemiosmosis (page 3). The energy released by the electron transport chain is used to pump hydrogen ions into the space between the two membranes of the mitochondrial envelope. The concentration of hydrogen ions in the intermembrane space

	ATP used	ATP made	Net gain ATP
Glycolysis	2	4	+2
Link reaction	–	–	–
Krebs cycle		2	+2
Oxidative phosphorylation		34	+34
	−2	40	+38

● **Table 2.1** Balance sheet of ATP use and synthesis for each molecule of glucose entering respiration.

becomes higher than that in the mitochondrial matrix, so a concentration gradient is set up. Hydrogen ions pass back into the mitochondrial matrix through protein channels in the inner membrane. Associated with each channel is the enzyme ATP synthetase. As the ions pass through the channel, their electrical potential energy is used to synthesise ATP *(figure 1.5)*.

The sequence of events in respiration and their sites are shown in *figure 2.5*. The balance sheet of ATP use and synthesis for each molecule of glucose entering the respiration pathway is shown in *table 2.1*.

SAQ 2.2

Calculate the number of reduced NAD and reduced FAD molecules produced for each molecule of glucose entering the respiration pathway when oxygen is available.

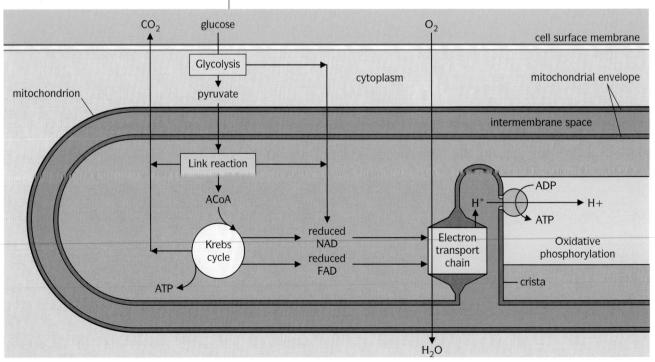

● **Figure 2.5** The sites of the events of respiration in a cell.

SAQ 2.3 ——————————
Using your answer to SAQ 2.2, calculate the number of ATP molecules produced for each molecule of glucose in oxidative phosphorylation.

SAQ 2.4 ——————————
Explain why the important contribution of the Krebs cycle to cellular energetics is the release of hydrogens and not the direct production of ATP.

Mitochondrial structure and function

In eukaryotic organisms, the mitochondrion is the site of the Krebs cycle and the electron transport chain. Mitochondria are rod-shaped or filamentous organelles about $0.5–1.0\,\mu m$ in diameter. Time-lapse photography shows that they are not rigid, but can change their shape. The number of mitochondria in a cell depends on its activity. Mammalian liver cells contain between 1000 and 2000 mitochondria, occupying 20% of the cell volume.

The structure of a mitochondrion is shown in *figure 2.6*. Like a chloroplast, each mitochondrion is surrounded by an **envelope** of two phospholipid membranes *(Foundation Biology)*. The outer membrane is smooth, but the inner is much folded inwards to form **cristae**. These give the inner membrane a large total surface area. Cristae in mitochondria from different types of cells show considerable variation, but, in general, mito-chondria from active cells have longer, more densely packed cristae than those from less active cells. The two membranes have different composi-tions and properties. The outer membrane is relatively permeable to small molecules, whilst the inner membrane is less permeable. The inner membrane is studded with tiny spheres, about $9\,nm$ in diameter, which are attached to the inner membrane by stalks *(figure 2.7)*. The spheres act as an ATPase and the whole complex of sphere and stalk is called **ATP synthetase**.

The inner membrane is the site of the electron transport chain and contains the proteins necessary for this. The space between the two membranes of the envelope usually has a lower pH than the matrix of the mitochondrion as a result of the hydrogen ions that are released into the intermem-brane space by the activity of the electron trans-port chain.

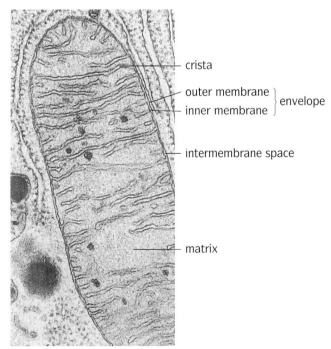

● *Figure 2.6* TEM of a mitochondrion from a pancreas ($\times\,15000$)

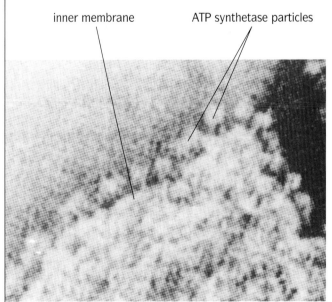

● *Figure 2.7* TEM of ATP synthetase particles on the inner membrane of a mitochondrion.

The **matrix** of the mitochondrion is the site of the link reaction and the Krebs cycle, and contains the enzymes needed for these reactions. It also contains small **ribosomes** and several identical copies of looped mitochondrial **DNA**.

ATP is formed in the matrix by the activity of ATP synthetase on the cristae. The energy for the production of ATP comes from the hydrogen ion gradient between the intermembrane space and the matrix. The ATP can be used for all the energy-requiring reactions of the cell, both inside and outside the mitochondrion.

SAQ 2.5

Explain how the structure of a mitochondrion is adapted for its functions in aerobic respiration.

Anaerobic respiration

When free oxygen is not present, hydrogen cannot be disposed of by combination with oxygen. The electron transfer chain therefore stops working and no further ATP is formed by oxidative phosphory-lation. If a cell is to gain even the two ATP molecules for each glucose yielded by glycolysis, it is essential to pass on the hydrogens from the reduced NAD which are also made in glycolysis. There are two different anaerobic pathways which solve the problem of 'dumping' hydrogen. Both pathways take place in the cytoplasm of the cell.

In various microorganisms such as yeast, and in some plant tissues, the hydrogen from reduced NAD is passed to ethanal (CH_3CHO). This releases the NAD and allows glycolysis to continue. The pathway is shown in *figure 2.8*. First, pyruvate is decarboxylated to ethanal; then the ethanal is reduced to ethanol. The conversion of glucose to ethanol is referred to as **alcoholic fermentation**.

In other microorganisms, and in mammalian muscles when deprived of oxygen, pyruvate acts as the hydrogen acceptor and is converted to lactate. Again, the NAD is released and allows glycolysis to continue in anaerobic conditions. This pathway is shown in *figure 2.9*.

These reactions 'buy time'. They allow the continued production of at least some ATP even

though oxygen is not available as the hydrogen acceptor. However, since the products of anaerobic reaction, ethanol or lactate, are toxic, the reactions cannot continue indefinitely. The pathway leading to ethanol cannot be reversed and the remaining chemical potential energy of ethanol is wasted. The lactate pathway can be reversed in mammals. Lactate is carried by the blood plasma to the liver and converted back to pyruvate. The liver oxidises some (20%) of the incoming lactate to carbon dioxide and water via aerobic respiration when oxygen is available again. The remainder of the lactate is converted by the liver to glycogen. The oxygen needed to allow this removal of lactate is called the **oxygen debt**.

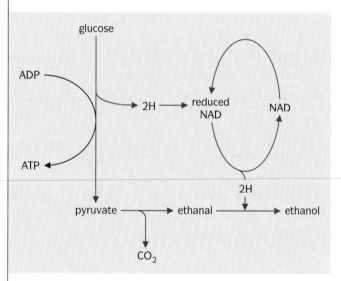

● *Figure 2.8* Anaerobic respiration: the ethanol pathway.

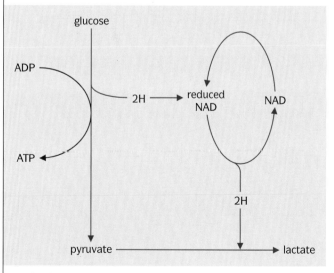

● *Figure 2.9* Anaerobic respiration: the lactate pathway.

SUMMARY

■ Respiration is the sequence of enzyme-controlled steps by which an organic molecule, usually glucose, is broken down so that its chemical potential energy can be used to make the energy currency, ATP.

■ In aerobic respiration, the sequence involves four main stages: glycolysis, the link reaction, the Krebs cycle and oxidative phosphorylation.

■ In glycolysis, glucose is first phosphorylated and then split into two triose phosphate molecules. These are further oxidised to pyruvate, giving a small yield of ATP and reduced NAD. Glycolysis occurs in the cell cytoplasm.

■ When oxygen is available (aerobic respiration), the pyruvate passes to the matrix of a mitochondrion. There, in the link reaction, it is decarboxylated and dehydrogenated and the remaining acetyl unit combined with coenzyme A to give acetylcoenzyme A.

■ The acetylcoenzyme A enters the Krebs cycle and donates the acetyl unit to oxaloacetate (4C) to make citrate (6C). The Krebs cycle decarboxylates and dehydrogenates citrate to oxaloacetate in a series of small steps. The oxaloacetate can then react with another acetylcoenzyme A from the link reaction.

■ Dehydrogenation provides hydrogen atoms which are accepted by the carriers NAD and FAD. These pass to the inner membrane of the mitochondrial envelope where the hydrogens are split into hydrogen ions and electrons,

■ The electrons are passed along a series of carriers. Some of the energy released in this process is used to phosphorylate ADP to ATP. The phosphorylation depends on a gradient of hydrogen ions set up across the inner membrane of the mitochondrial envelope by chemiosmosis.

■ At the end of the carrier chain, electrons and protons are recombined and reduce oxygen to water.

■ In the absence of oxygen as a hydrogen acceptor, a small yield of ATP is made by dumping hydrogen into other pathways in the cytoplasm which produce ethanol or lactate.

Questions

1 Discuss the parts played in aerobic respiration by:
   a the phosphorylation of glucose;
   b acetylcoenzyme A;
   c the oxidative decarboxylation of pyruvate;
   d the electron transfer chain.

2 Explain why anaerobic respiration produces much less available energy than aerobic respiration.

3 a Outline the biochemical pathways by which energy is released from glucose in anaerobic conditions.
   b State what happens to the products of anaerobic respiration when oxygen becomes available.

4 Describe oxidative phosphorylation and distinguish it from oxidative decarboxylation.

5 Describe the function of the various enzymes involved in respiration.

6 Outline the synthesis of ATP in respiration.

Chapter three

Energy and ecosystems

By the end of this chapter you should be able to:

1 define the terms *habitat*, *niche*, *population*, *community* and *ecosystem*, and describe examples of each;

2 state that energy flows through an ecosystem, whereas matter tends to cycle within it;

3 explain the roles of photosynthesis and respiration in the transfer of energy into, through and out of an ecosystem;

4 explain the terms *producer*, *consumer* and *trophic level*, and state examples of these in specific food chains and food webs;

5 explain how energy losses occur along food chains, and understand what is meant by *efficiency* of transfer;

6 understand how to construct and interpret pyramids of biomass and pyramids of energy;

7 describe the carbon cycle;

8 discuss the ways in which human activities, especially burning fossil fuels and deforestation, may affect the balance of the carbon cycle, and consider what can be done to reduce possible harmful consequences;

9 describe the nitrogen cycle;

10 discuss the ways in which the overuse of nitrogen-containing fertilisers may affect the balance of the nitrogen cycle, and consider the viability of alternatives to the use of such fertilisers.

So far in this book, we have looked in detail at two fundamentally important processes which occur inside living cells, that is photosynthesis and respiration. From this molecule-sized view of living organisms, we will go to the other end of the scale and look at the interactions of whole communities of organisms and the environment around them. This branch of biology is called **ecology**.

In moving from the very small to the very large in this way, you will need to become familiar with several new terms. It is important that you use them correctly right from the start, because each one has a precise meaning, and you will be misunderstood if you do not realise this. Special care is needed with these terms, because they all sound familiar from everyday use, and it is easy to think you already know what they mean when perhaps you do not.

A **habitat** is *a place where an organism lives*. The habitat of an oak tree might be the edge of an area of deciduous woodland. The habitat of a leaf-mining caterpillar might be inside a leaf on the oak tree.

A **population** is *a group of organisms of the same species, which live in the same place at the same time, and can interbreed with each other*. All of the oak trees in the wood, for example, make up a population of oak trees. However, if the oak trees in a nearby wood can interbreed with those in the first wood, then they too belong to the same population.

A **community** is *all the organisms, of all the different species, living in a habitat*. The woodland community includes all the plants – oak trees, ash trees, grasses, hawthorn bushes, bluebells and so on – all the microorganisms and larger fungi, and all the animals which live in the wood.

An **ecosystem** is *a relatively self-contained, interacting community of organisms, and the environment in which they live and with which they interact*. Thus the woodland ecosystem includes not only the community of organisms, but also the soil, the water in the rain and streams, the air, the rocks and anything else which is in the wood. As you will see later in this chapter, energy flows into the ecosystem from outside it (as sunlight), flows through the organisms in the ecosystem (as food) and eventually leaves the ecosystem (as heat). Matter, on the other hand – that is, atoms and molecules of substances such as carbon and nitrogen – cycles round an ecosystem, where some atoms are reused over and over again by different organisms.

No ecosystem is entirely self-contained; organisms, energy and matter in one ecosystem do interact with those from other ecosystems.

Nevertheless, the concept is a useful one, because it allows you to focus on something of a manageable size.

You can think of ecosystems on different scales. You could consider the surface of a rotting crab apple to be an ecosystem, with its own community of moulds and other organisms, or you could think of the whole hedgerow in which the crab apple tree is growing as an ecosystem.

The **niche** of an organism is *its role in the ecosystem*. The niche of an oak tree is as a producer of carbohydrates and other organic substances which provide food for other organisms in the ecosystem. It takes carbon dioxide from the air and returns oxygen to it. Its roots penetrate deeply into the soil, where they take up water and minerals. Water vapour diffuses from its leaves into the air. These leaves provide habitats for myriads of insects and other animals. It is almost impossible to provide a complete description of the niche of any organism, because there are so many ways in which it interacts with other components of the ecosystem of which it is a part.

Energy flow through an ecosystem

In chapters 1 and 2, you have seen that living organisms need a constant supply of energy to maintain cellular activities and therefore to stay alive. This energy supply comes from organic chemicals such as carbohydrates, from which it is transferred by respiration. The carbohydrates are produced by photosynthesis, which converts energy from certain wavelengths of sunlight into chemical energy.

Green plants and other photosynthetic organisms therefore have the essential role of providing the entire input of energy to an ecosystem. They are **producers**. The carbohydrates and other organic chemicals which they synthesise serve as supplies of chemical energy to all of the other organisms in the ecosystem. These other organisms, which include all the animals and fungi, and many of the microorganisms, consume the organic chemicals made by plants. They are **consumers**.

Food chains and food webs

The way in which energy flows from producer to consumers can be shown by drawing a **food chain**. Arrows in the food chain indicate the direction in which the energy flows. A simple food chain in a deciduous wood could be:

oak tree → winter moth caterpillar → great tit → sparrowhawk

In this food chain, the oak tree is the producer, and the three animals are consumers. The caterpillar is a **primary consumer**, the great tit a **secondary consumer** and the sparrowhawk a **tertiary consumer**.

These different positions in a food chain are called **trophic levels**. 'Trophic' means 'feeding'.

Within this woodland ecosystem, there will be a large number of such food chains. The interrelationships between many food chains can be drawn as a **food web**. *Figure 3.1* shows a partial food web for such an ecosystem. You can pick out many different food chains within this web.

You may notice that a particular animal does not always occupy the same position in a food chain. While herbivores such as caterpillars and rabbits tend *always* to be herbivores, and therefore always primary consumers, carnivores often feed at several different trophic levels in different food chains. Thus the fox is a primary consumer when it eats a fallen crab apple, a secondary consumer when it eats a rabbit, and a tertiary consumer when it eats a great tit. Animals which regularly feed as both primary and higher-level consumers, such as humans, are known as omnivores.

The food web also shows the importance of a group of organisms called **decomposers**. Most decomposers live in the soil, and their role in an ecosystem is to feed on dead organisms and waste material, such as dead leaves, faeces and urine. You can see that energy from *every* organism in the ecosystem flows into the decomposers. Decomposers include many bacteria, fungi, and also some larger animals such as earthworms. Sometimes, the term 'decomposer' is used only for bacteria and fungi, which feed

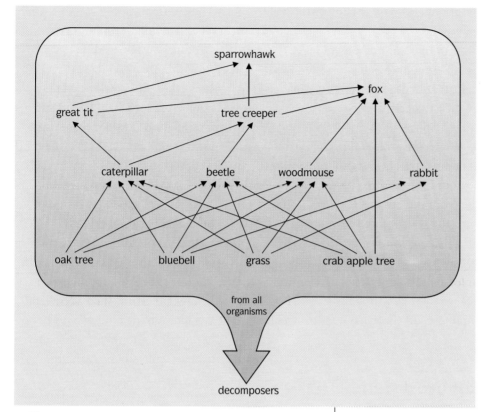

● **Figure 3.1** A food web in oak woodland.

saprotrophically, while the larger animals are called **detritivores**. Decomposers are a largely unseen but vitally important group within every ecosystem. You will find out more about their roles in the carbon and nitrogen cycles on pages 27–35.

Energy losses along food chains

Whenever energy is transferred from one form, or from one system, to another some is always lost as heat. As energy passes along a food chain, large losses from the food chain occur at each transfer, both within and between the organisms. *Figure 3.2* shows these losses for a simple food chain.

Of the sunlight falling onto the ecosystem, only a very small percentage is converted by the green plants into chemical energy. In most ecosystems, the plants convert less than 3% of this sunlight to chemical energy. The reasons for this inefficiency include:

■ some sunlight missing leaves entirely, and falling onto the ground or other nonphoto-synthesising surfaces;

■ some sunlight being reflected from the surfaces of leaves;

■ some sunlight passing through leaves, without being trapped by chlorophyll molecules;

■ only certain wavelengths of light being absorbed by chlorophyll;

■ energy losses as energy absorbed by chlorophyll is transferred along the pathways of the light-dependent reactions and the Calvin cycle.

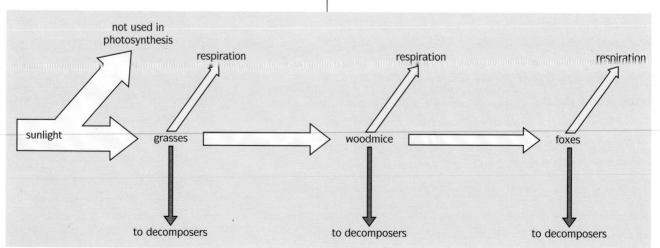

● **Figure 3.2** Energy losses in a food chain.

The chemical potential energy, now in the plants' tissues, is contained in various organic molecules, especially carbohydrates, fats and proteins. It is from these molecules that the primary consumers in the ecosystem obtain their energy supply. However, in most plants, almost half of the chemical potential energy stored by plants is used by the plants themselves. They release the energy by respiration, using it for purposes such as active transport. During these processes, much energy is lost to the environment as heat.

What is left is then available for other organisms, which feed on the plants. Once again, losses occur between the plants and the primary consumers. The reasons for these losses include:

■ not all of the parts of the plants being available to be eaten, such as woody tissues and some roots;
■ not all of the parts of the plants eaten being digestible, so that not all of the molecules can be absorbed and used by the primary consumer;
■ energy losses as heat within the consumer's digestive system, as food is digested.

As a result of the loss of energy during respiration in the plants, and the three reasons listed above, the overall efficiency of transfer of energy from producer to primary consumer is rarely greater than 10%.

Similar losses occur at each trophic level. So, as energy is passed along a food chain, less and less energy is available at each successive trophic level. Food chains rarely have more than four or five links in them because there simply would not be sufficient energy left to support animals so far removed from the original energy input to the producers. If you *can* pick out a five-organism food chain from a food web, you will probably find that the 'top' carnivore also feeds at a lower level in a different food chain.

SAQ 3.1

Energy losses from mammals and birds tend to be significantly greater than those from other organisms. Suggest why this is so.

Productivity

The rate at which plants convert light energy into chemical potential energy is called **productivity**, or **primary productivity**. It is usually measured in kilojoules of energy transferred per square metre per year ($kJ\,m^{-2}\,year^{-1}$).

Gross primary productivity is the total quantity of energy converted by plants in this way. **Net primary productivity** is the energy which remains as chemical energy after the plants have supplied their own needs in respiration.

SAQ 3.2

Table 3.1 shows some information about energy transfers in three ecosystems.

a Calculate the figures for respiration by plants in the alfalfa field, and the net primary productivity of the young pine forest.

b How much energy is available to the primary consumers in the rain forest?

c Suggest why the gross primary productivity of the rain forest is so much greater than that of the pine forest. (There are many reasons – think of as many as you can.)

d Suggest why the net primary productivity of the alfalfa field is greater than that of the rain forest. (Again, you may be able to think of several reasons.)

	Mature rain forest in Puerto Rico	*Alfalfa field in USA*	*Young pine forest in England*
Gross primary productivity /$kJ\,m^{-2}\,year^{-1}$	188 000	102 000	51 000
Respiration by plants /$kJ\,m^{-2}\,year^{-1}$	134 000		20 000
Net primary productivity /$kJ\,m^{-2}\,year^{-1}$	54 000	64 000	

● Table 3.1

Pyramids of biomass and energy

If you could collect all the living organisms in an ecosystem, and measure their mass, you would probably find that the mass of producers is considerably greater than the mass of primary consumers, which in turn is greater than the mass of secondary consumers, and so on. This has been done (it is a very complex and time-consuming operation if done thoroughly) for several ecosystems. Two examples are shown in *figure 3.3*.

These diagrams are called **pyramids of biomass**. 'Biomass' simply means the mass of living organisms; it is measured as dry mass, which is the mass of the organisms after all water has been removed from their bodies. The area of each box in the pyramid represents the quantity of mass at that trophic level.

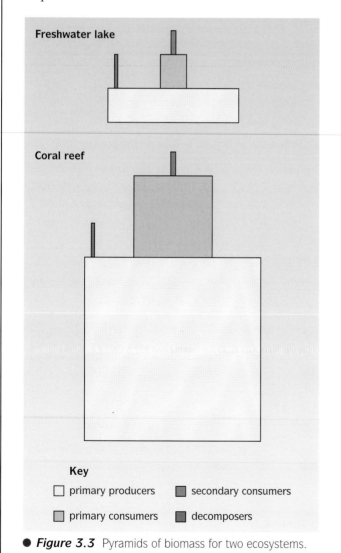

Key

☐ primary producers   ▨ secondary consumers

▨ primary consumers   ▨ decomposers

● ***Figure 3.3*** Pyramids of biomass for two ecosystems.

SAQ 3.3

Table 3.2 shows the biomass of the organisms at different trophic levels in a short stretch of a river. Draw an accurate pyramid of biomass, on graph paper, for these data.

Trophic level	Total biomass/g
primary consumers	124
secondary consumers	42
tertiary consumers	14

● **Table 3.2**

As you move up a pyramid of biomass, the boxes get progressively smaller. This is because the progressive loss of energy as it passes along a food chain results in less being available to supply animals feeding at higher trophic levels. The sunlight falling onto an ecosystem is sufficient to supply a large quantity of plant tissue with its energy requirements, but by the time the energy has been passed on to the primary consumers a great deal has been lost, so less animal tissue can be supplied with the energy it needs. A pyramid of biomass helps you to visualise the size of these energy losses, because they are roughly indicated by the reduction in size of the boxes as you move up from one trophic level to the next.

An even better way of showing these losses graphically is to draw a **pyramid of energy**. Here, the actual *energy content* of the organisms in the ecosystem is measured. This is done by drying a sample of each species of organism, burning it in a calorimeter, and measuring the quantity of energy released per gram. As you can imagine, this is very time consuming, and not a particularly pleasant thing to do to an animal, so ecologists normally refer to records of mean energy content for the species they are working with, rather than measuring energy content directly. The energy content per gram for each species is then multiplied by its biomass, to calculate the total energy content of the population of that species in the ecosystem. Energy contents of all the species at each trophic level are then added to arrive at the final figure.

When calculated in this way, the figures obtained represent the energy content of each trophic level at a particular moment in time. *Figure 3.4a* shows a pyramid of energy drawn from this type of data, for a freshwater ecosystem.

A much more useful measurement is the *rate* at which energy flows through each trophic level. You have already met this idea on page 25; gross primary productivity is the rate at which energy flows through the first trophic level. If rates of energy flow are calculated for each trophic level, in units such as kilojoules per square metre per year, then a **pyramid of energy flow**, such as the one in *figure 3.4b*, can be drawn.

SAQ 3.4

Figure 3.4a is a pyramid of energy for a freshwater lake. The area of each box represents the quantity of energy contained in the organisms living under one square metre of the lake surface, in kJ m^{-2}.

a Calculate the quantity of energy in the primary consumers. (The diagram is drawn to scale.)

b Compare *figure 3.4a* with *3.4b*, which is a pyramid of energy flow for the same ecosystem. What differences are there in the shape of the two pyramids? Suggest reasons for these differences.

The carbon cycle

Living organisms require not only a supply of *energy*, but also a supply of *matter* from which to build their bodies. The elements from which this matter is made are mostly hydrogen, carbon and oxygen, which are contained in all the organic molecules within organisms. Proteins and nucleotides (page 41) also contain nitrogen, and some proteins contain sulphur. Phosphorus is an important component of nucleotides. Other elements are needed in smaller quantities, such as magnesium, calcium, iodine and iron.

Atoms of these elements are used over and over again within an ecosystem, or passed into other ecosystems. They are passed from one organism to another, cycling round through the different living organisms, and also through the non-living parts of the ecosystem, such as the air, soil, water and rocks. Imagine a carbon atom in a molecule of phospholipid in a cell membrane in a cell in your little finger. It might at one time have been part of Henry VIII, or a rat, or a boa constrictor at some stage, before being breathed out into the air as carbon dioxide, taken in by a plant, made into a starch molecule and then eaten by you.

Figure 3.5 shows the routes a carbon atom can take as it moves within and between ecosystems.

SAQ 3.5

a What is the only process which removes carbon dioxide from the air in a terrestrial ecosystem?

b Describe one pathway by which a carbon atom in a limestone sediment under the sea could become part of a molecule in a person.

As far as living organisms are concerned, photosynthesis removes carbon dioxide from the air and respiration returns carbon dioxide to the air. Over a year, these two processes come very close to a perfect balance; in other words, the

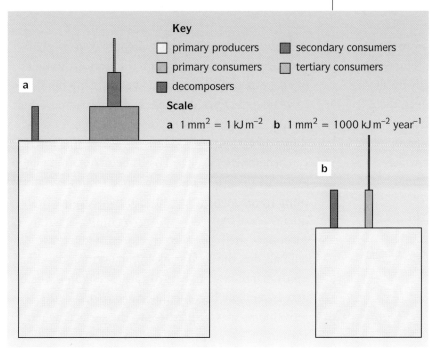

Key
☐ primary producers   ■ secondary consumers
■ primary consumers   ☐ tertiary consumers
■ decomposers

Scale
a 1 mm^2 = 1 kJ m^{-2} **b** 1 mm^2 = 1000 kJ m^{-2} year^{-1}

● *Figure 3.4* Pyramids of **a** energy at one moment in time and **b** rate of energy flow for a freshwater ecosystem.

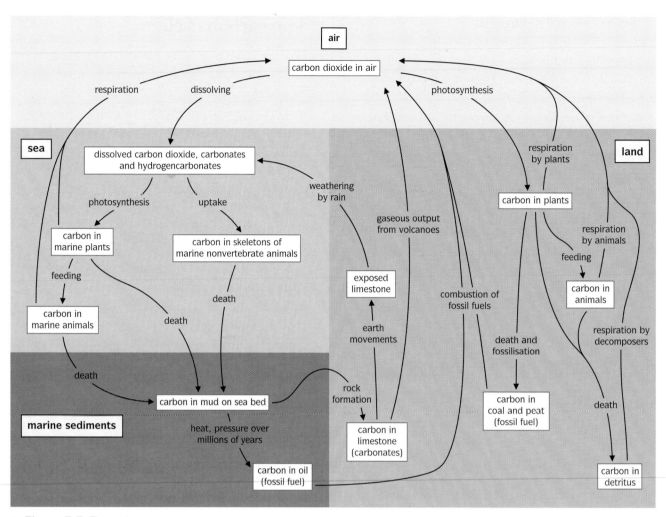

● *Figure 3.5* The carbon cycle.

total amount of carbon dioxide removed from the air by green plants is equalled by the amount returned partly by these same green plants, and partly by all consumers, including decomposers. However, there are seasonal fluctuations in atmospheric carbon dioxide levels in many areas of the world, partly because rates of photosynthesis vary more widely with seasonal changes than rates of respiration.

SAQ 3.6

a   At which time of year would you expect the carbon dioxide concentration in the atmosphere above Britain to be greatest, assuming that fluctuations in carbon dioxide concentration are caused by variations in rates of photosynthesis?

b   Suggest one other possible source of variation in atmospheric carbon dioxide concentration between winter and summer.

However, not all carbon dioxide fixed by plants is returned to the air through respiration. Some plants, especially trees, may live for many hundreds of years, effectively locking up fixed carbon in their tissues. In boggy soils, decomposers do not break down all carbon compounds, and large quantities can accumulate as peat. Fossil fuels containing large amounts of carbon may be formed from the bodies of plants or microorganisms. In the sea, significant quantities of carbon become part of the calcium carbonate shells of nonvertebrates. When these animals die, the shells sink to the bottom, building up over millions of years to form sediments which may eventually become limestone rocks. Earth movements may bring these to the surface, where various processes release carbon dioxide from the carbonates which they contain.

Carbon dioxide and the greenhouse effect

As well as providing the major source of carbon dioxide for photosynthesis, the carbon dioxide in the atmosphere has another important function. *Figure 3.6* shows how carbon dioxide, and other so-called 'greenhouse gases' such as water vapour and methane, in the atmosphere trap outgoing long-wave radiation and so keep the Earth warmer than it would otherwise be. Short-wave radiation from the Sun passes freely through the atmosphere, much of it reaching the ground. Some of this radiation is re-emitted from the ground as longer-wave radiation, including infrared. These longer wavelengths do not all pass through the 'greenhouse gases'. Quite a high proportion is reflected back towards the Earth.

This is called the **greenhouse effect**, because it has some similarities with the way in which the glass of a greenhouse keeps the air inside warmer than the air outside. Without the greenhouse effect, the Earth would be too cold to support life. It would be a frozen, lifeless planet.

Human effects on the carbon cycle

Global warming

In recent years, there has been growing concern about the increasing concentration of carbon dioxide in the atmosphere. It is growing at a rate of about 1.5 parts per million per year. Since the late 1950s, carbon dioxide levels have been monitored at the Mauna Loa Observatory in Hawaii. They have risen from about 316 parts per million in 1958 to 355 parts per million in 1993. There is concern about this because of the possibility of **global warming**.

As atmospheric carbon dioxide concentration rises, we would expect the quantity of long-wave radiation which is trapped to increase, which would result in an increase in the mean temperature of the Earth. So far, no incontrovertible and universally accepted evidence has been found that such a rise in temperature is taking place, although there is clear evidence that past changes in carbon dioxide concentrations have indeed been accompanied by

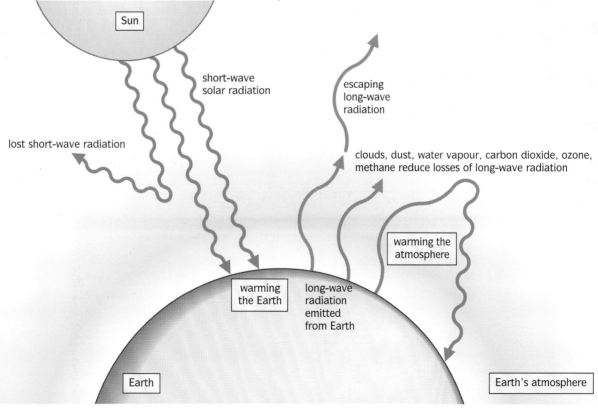

● *Figure 3.6* The greenhouse effect.

changes in global temperature (*figure 3.7*). This, together with our knowledge of how carbon dioxide contributes to the greenhouse effect, suggests (though does not prove) that increasing carbon dioxide concentrations may cause increased global temperatures. Despite these uncertainties, the potential effects of such a change in the Earth's climate are so wide-ranging, so large and so unpredictable that most people feel that we cannot afford to be complacent.

For example, a rise in global temperature could melt ice at the north and south poles, which could cause sea levels to rise. This could result in extensive flooding, and many low-lying areas of land would disappear under the sea.

Rising temperatures could also affect climate, and therefore change the current distribution of plant and animal communities. Arctic communities, for example, might disappear, as plants and animals adapted to these harsh conditions are unable to compete successfully with other organisms which can cope better with warmer climates. However, it is quite impossible to predict just how global warming might affect climates in particular parts of the world. Each computer simulation which scientists have run seems to come up with a different answer. Will the Sahara become even hotter and drier, or will it rain more? Will cyclones over the Caribbean become even more violent, or will they drift further northward, threatening wide areas of North America which rarely

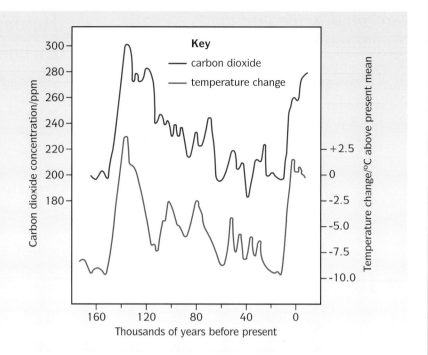

● **Figure 3.7** Variations in carbon dioxide concentrations in the atmosphere, and mean global temperature, during the last 160 000 years.

experience such extreme weather now? No-one knows for certain.

Agriculture could also be affected. Warmer winters in Britain, for example, could affect the numbers and distribution of pest species such as aphids. These could survive the winter in larger numbers, breed faster and earlier and infest crops on a larger scale than they do at present. Aphids carry viral diseases, which could therefore become more widespread and reduce crop yields. However, we have no proof that this might happen. It could be that ladybird populations would also increase and keep aphid populations at reasonable levels.

On the other hand, there could be some positive changes. Higher concentrations of carbon dioxide could increase rates of photosynthesis, both in crop plants, which would provide more food for people, and in natural ecosystems. Warmer temperatures in Britain could mean that we could grow new crops, such as soya beans. However, here again we do not really know exactly what might happen; we can do little more than guess.

Fossil fuel combustion and deforestation

The rise in carbon dioxide concentrations in recent years may well have been caused by human activities. The main cause seems to be the increased burning of fossil fuels. A secondary cause could be the destruction of forests.

When fossil fuels are burnt, carbon which would otherwise have remained locked up in the Earth is released into the air as carbon dioxide. In 1993, the mass of carbon returned to the atmosphere by combustion of fossil fuels all over the world was estimated to be just over 5×10^{15} g. The great majority of these emissions comes from industrialised countries, where fuel is burnt to produce electricity, to power vehicles, such as cars and aeroplanes, and industrial processes, and for heating.

The impact of deforestation on carbon dioxide levels is much debated. A *mature* forest tree takes almost the same amount of carbon dioxide from the air in photosynthesis, as is returned to the air by respiration. Therefore, simply cutting down mature trees has little if any effect on carbon dioxide levels. This is especially true if the land on which the tree was growing is subsequently planted with crops. These may photosynthesise rapidly and actually remove *more* carbon dioxide from the air, although subsequent eating of these crops, followed by respiration, will return the carbon dioxide to the air once more. However, if the land is cleared by burning, then carbon locked up in the wood of the trees is released suddenly as carbon dioxide.

The uncertainty about deforestation and carbon dioxide levels is only one of many unanswered questions about the issue of global warming. For example, if you look at *figure 3.7* you can see that there have been very large fluctuations in carbon dioxide levels in the past, long before humans began burning fossil fuels in large quantities. We do not know for certain what caused these fluctuations, but it was not human activities. This indicates that there is much that we do not know about the factors influencing the concentration of carbon dioxide in the atmosphere. However, you will probably also notice that the current levels are the highest they have been for the last 100 000 years, indicating that perhaps we really do have something to worry about.

Measures to reduce carbon dioxide emissions

Despite, or perhaps because of, so many unanswered questions, there is almost universal agreement that we should attempt to reduce carbon dioxide emissions as quickly as possible. In June 1992, in Rio de Janeiro in Brazil, the British Prime Minister John

Major and the leaders of 150 other countries signed a document called the *Framework Convention on Climate Change*. This committed the United Kingdom and other countries to recognising and addressing the issue of rising carbon dioxide levels.

The stated aim of the United Kingdom Government is to reduce carbon dioxide emissions to 1990 levels by the year 2000. This may not seem very ambitious, but political and economical arguments have made it difficult to contemplate reducing carbon dioxide emissions by anything like as much as ecologists would like to see. In 1990, it is estimated that these emissions were 158 megatonnes of carbon. By 2000, without measures being taken to prevent an increase, they could be as high as 180 megatonnes. The achievement of even this stabilisation would be a tremendous success. It is also important to realise that the 1990 levels were much lower than those in 1970 (*figure 3.8*), so we are already producing much less carbon dioxide than we were doing 20 years ago.

The main ways in which the British Government hopes to achieve these reductions are by:

■ encouraging more efficient use of energy in the home and by businesses, including electrical energy, because much of our electricity is generated by burning fossil fuels;

■ encouraging changes in the way that electricity is generated, such as continuing to produce 20% of our electricity by nuclear power and introducing more Combined Heat and Power generating stations, which make more efficient use of the fuel they burn;

■ setting energy-efficient standards for domestic appliances;

■ changing building regulations to ensure that new houses, offices and public buildings are more energy-efficient;

■ increasing duties on petrol and diesel fuel, to try to reduce their consumption.

As well as reducing carbon dioxide emissions, the British Government aims to conserve soils and forests, both of which hold large quantities of carbon. Peat soils hold the greatest mass of carbon per hectare, while light agricultural soils hold the

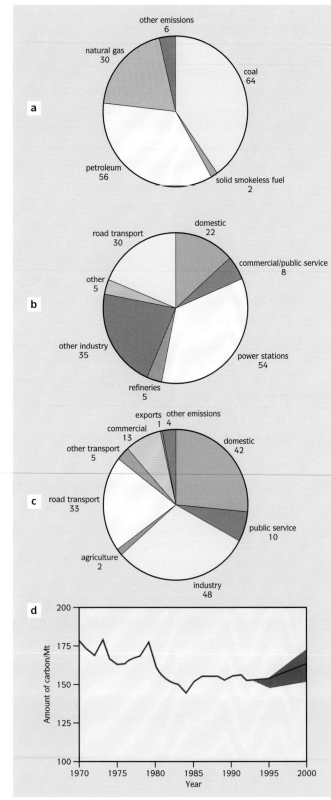

● **Figure 3.8** Carbon dioxide emissions in the UK, in 1990 **a** by type of fuel, **b** by emission sources and **c** by end users. The figures show the amount of carbon emitted, in millions of tonnes. **d** UK carbon dioxide emissions between 1970 and 1992 and possible future trends.

least. At the moment, about 10% of the United Kingdom is covered by forest, and this is increasing. Tree cover has doubled since the beginning of the century. About 20 000 hectares of land is afforested each year, and the Government is supporting this trend by supplying grants for planting trees.

Will these measures be enough? Most environmentalists say that they will not. They would like to see a different transport policy, which would encourage the use of public transport and discourage the use of private vehicles. They would like to see more use of energy sources which do not emit carbon dioxide, such as wind, solar, wave and tidal power. At the moment, these changes do not seem to be politically achievable in the United Kingdom. However, even our present position is a great step forward compared with the 1960s and 1970s, and perhaps as people become more aware of the issues involved, it will become possible to make more radical changes in the way we live, to reduce the emissions of greenhouse gases even more.

The combustion of fossil fuels and deforestation cause several other environmental problems, besides the imbalances in the carbon cycle described above. These include the production of acid rain, soil erosion, and loss of habitats and species diversity. You can read more about this in *Ecology and Conservation* in this series.

The nitrogen cycle

Nitrogen is an essential element for all living organisms, because it is found in proteins and nucleic acids. There is far more nitrogen in the air than carbon; nitrogen gas makes up around 78% of the air, compared with only 0.04% carbon dioxide. However, whereas carbon dioxide is readily fixed by photosynthetic organisms, the fixation of nitrogen is far less easy. This is because nitrogen gas exists as molecular nitrogen, in which two nitrogen atoms are covalently bonded. In this form, nitrogen is very unreactive. With each breath, you take in around 350 cm^3 of nitrogen gas, but this is completely useless to you. It simply passes in and out of your body unchanged.

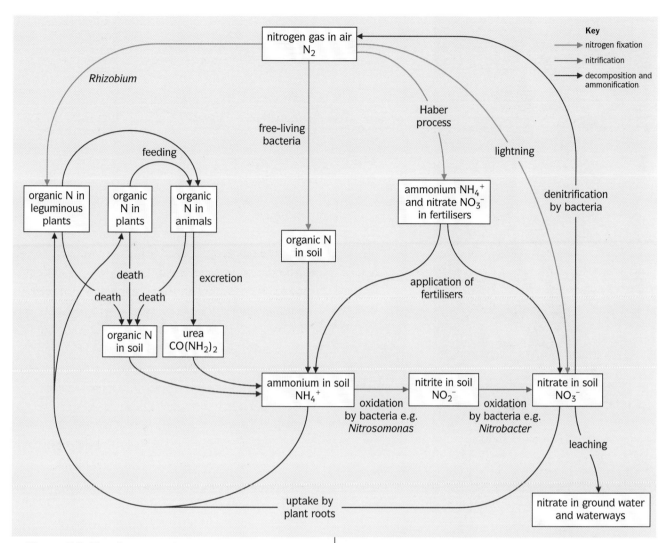

● **Figure 3.9** The nitrogen cycle.

Nitrogen fixation

Fixation by living organisms

The fixation of nitrogen is carried out by prokaryotes. Several species of bacteria and blue-greens fix nitrogen. One of the best-known nitrogen-fixing bacteria is *Rhizobium*. This bacterium lives freely in the soil, and also in the roots of many species of plants, especially leguminous plants (belonging to the pea family, such as peas, beans, clover, alfalfa and acacia trees). *Rhizobium* can only fix nitrogen in conditions where oxygen is not present, and appears only to be able to do this to a very limited extent when living freely in the soil. Most nitrogen fixation by *Rhizobium* occurs when it is living in plant roots.

Rhizobium is found in most soils. When a leguminous plant germinates, its roots produce proteins called lectins which bind to polysaccharides on the cell surface of the bacteria. The bacteria invade the roots, spreading along the root hairs. They stimulate some of the cells in the root to divide and develop into small lumps or nodules, inside which the bacteria form colonies (*figure 3.10*).

The bacteria fix nitrogen with the help of an enzyme called **nitrogenase**. This enzyme catalyses the conversion of nitrogen gas, N_2, to ammonium ions, NH_4^+. To do this, it needs:

■ a supply of hydrogen;
■ a supply of ATP;
■ anaerobic conditions.

The hydrogen comes from reduced NADP which is produced by the plant. The ATP comes from the metabolism of sucrose, produced by photosynthesis

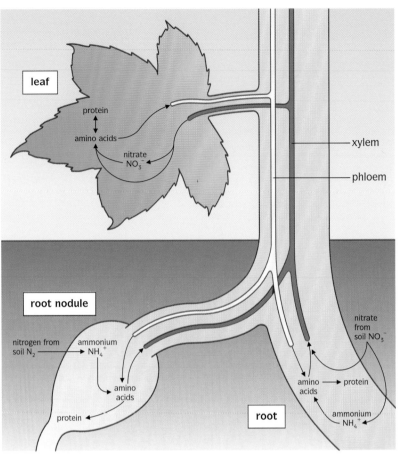

● **Figure 3.11** A summary of nitrogen metabolism and transport in plants.

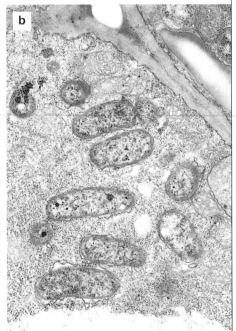

● **Figure 3.10**

a Root nodules, containing nitrogen-fixing bacteria, on clover roots.

b EM (× 12000) of part of a cell in a root nodule. The oval structures are nitrogen-fixing bacteria, which are each enclosed by a membrane belonging to the plant cell. You can also see the cell wall, several mitochondria, endoplasmic reticulum and ribosomes in the plant cell.

in the plant's leaves and transported into the roots. In the root nodules, sucrose is converted to glucose phosphate, which is then used in glycolysis and the Krebs cycle to generate ATP. Anaerobic conditions are maintained through the production, by the plant, of a protein called leghaemoglobin. This, like myoglobin, has a high affinity for oxygen, and effectively 'mops up' oxygen which diffuses into the nodules. (The structures and functions of myoglobin and haemoglobin are described in *Foundation Biology* and *Transport, Regulation and Control* in this series.)

The relationship between the plant and the bacteria is therefore a very close one. The plant supplies living space, and the conditions required by the bacteria to fix nitrogen. The bacteria supply the plant with fixed nitrogen. This is an example of **mutualism**, in which two organisms of different species live very closely together, each meeting some of the other's needs.

Fixation in the atmosphere

When lightning passes through the atmosphere, the huge quantities of energy involved can cause nitrogen molecules to react with oxygen, forming nitrogen oxides. These dissolve in rain, and are carried to the ground. In countries where there are frequent thunderstorms, for example many tropical countries, this is a very significant source of fixed nitrogen.

Fixation by the Haber process

The production of fertilisers containing fixed nitrogen is a major industry. In the Haber process, nitrogen and hydrogen gases are reacted together to produce ammonia. This requires considerable energy inputs, so the resulting fertilisers are not cheap. The ammonia is often converted to ammonium nitrate, which is the most widely used inorganic fertiliser in the world.

Use of fixed nitrogen by plants

In legumes, the fixed nitrogen produced by *Rhizobium* in their root nodules is used to make **amino acids**. These are transported out of the nodules into xylem, distributed to all parts of the plant and used within cells to synthesise proteins.

Other plants rely on supplies of fixed nitrogen in the soil. Their root hairs take up **nitrate ions** by active transport. In many plants, the nitrate is reduced in the roots, producing first nitrite, then ammonia, and then amino acids which are transported to other parts of the plant in xylem. In other plant species, the nitrate ions are transported, in xylem, to the leaves before undergoing these processes. Again, most of the nitrogen ends up as part of protein molecules in the plant, especially in seeds and storage tissues.

Assimilation of nitrogen by animals

Animals, including humans, can only use nitrogen when it is part of an organic molecule. Most of our nitrogen supply comes from proteins in the diet, with a small amount from nucleic acids. During digestion, proteins are broken down to amino acids, before being absorbed into the blood and distributed to all cells in the body. Here they are built up again into proteins. Excess amino acids are deaminated in the liver, where the nitrogen becomes part of urea molecules. These are excreted in urine. (You can read more about these processes in *Foundation Biology* and *Transport, Regulation and Control*.)

Return of nitrate to the soil from living organisms

When an animal or plant dies, the proteins in its cells are gradually broken down to amino acids. This is done by **decomposers**, especially bacteria and fungi, which produce protease enzymes. The decomposers use some of the amino acids for their own growth, while some are broken down and the nitrogen released as ammonia. Ammonia is also produced from the urea in animal urine. The production of ammonia is called **ammonification**.

Ammonia in the soil is rapidly converted to nitrite ions, NO_2^-, and then nitrate ions, NO_3^-, by a group of bacteria called **nitrifying bacteria**. These bacteria derive their energy from this process. This is an oxidation process, and only occurs freely in well-aerated soils. Boggy soils are therefore often short of nitrates. Some plants have become adapted to growing in such soils by supplementing their nitrogen intake using animal protein. These carnivorous plants trap insects, whose proteins are digested and absorbed by the plant *(figure 3.12)*.

Denitrification

Denitrifying bacteria provide themselves with energy by reducing nitrate to nitrogen gas, which is returned to the air. They are common in places such as sewage treatment plants, compost heaps and wet soils.

● **Figure 3.12** The greater sundew, *Drosera anglica*, only grows in very wet soils where nitrates are in extremely short supply. The sticky glands on the leaves trap insects. The leaves then curl over, and digest and absorb nutrients, including amino acids, from the insect's body.

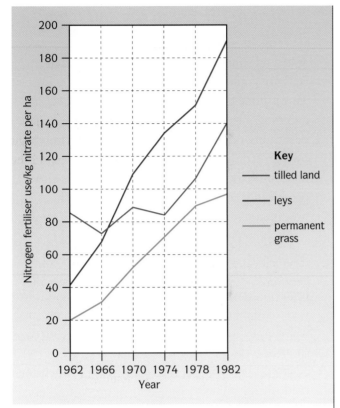

● **Figure 3.13** The use of nitrogen-containing fertilisers in England and Wales between 1962 and 1982. A ley is a meadow from which grass is harvested each year to make hay or silage.

Human effects on the nitrogen cycle

Nitrates in water

Figure 3.14 shows the levels of dissolved nitrate in the Great Ouse at Bedford, UK between 1957 and 1982. You can see that there is a long term trend of increasing nitrate concentrations in the river. The oscillations are caused by seasonal changes in rainfall. Nitrate is highly water-soluble, and is leached from soil and washed into the river from surrounding land in autumn and winter. In 1976, there was a long, hot, dry summer, and the nitrate levels in the Great Ouse fell. However, when it eventually rained in the autumn, there was an especially high peak in these levels.

What has caused this long-term increase in nitrate levels in fresh water? Initially, it was thought to be a direct result of the increasing application of inorganic fertilisers to arable land. It is now known, however, that the picture is not quite that simple. Inorganic fertilisers do contribute to nitrates in fresh water, but so do organic fertilisers such as manures. In fact, spreading animal manure on the land may cause more leaching of nitrates than spreading ammonium nitrate, partly because it is less easy for a farmer to calculate the correct amount to apply.

In a fertile soil, only about 5–8% of the nitrate is likely to have come from recently applied inorganic or organic fertilisers. Over 90% of the nitrate in the soil comes from the breakdown, by bacteria, of organic matter in the soil. A good soil may contain several thousand kilograms of nitrogen per hectare in humus, some of which is converted to nitrate each year by nitrifying bacteria.

Another major cause of the increased nitrate levels in water is the ploughing up of land on which grass has been growing for many years. Grassland on which animals are grazed accumulates large amounts of nitrates in the soil *(figure 3.15)*. When

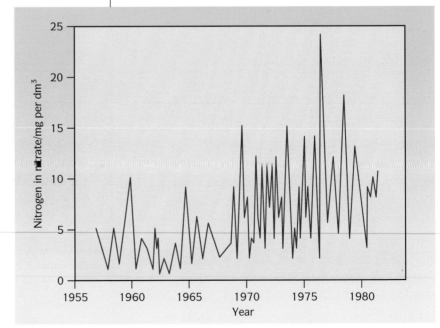

● **Figure 3.14** Nitrate concentrations in the River Ouse at Bedford, UK between 1957 and 1982.

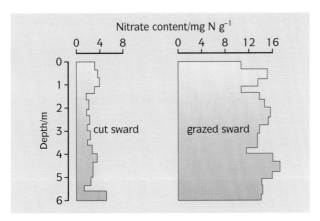

● **Figure 3.15** Nitrate content of soil at different depths beneath grassland which is harvested (cut sward) and grazed by sheep (grazed sward).

this is ploughed up, very significant amounts of nitrates can be washed out. This was done on a large scale in the Second World War, to help to produce more food. The 'half-life' of the store of nitrates in these ploughed soils is around 40 years, so we are still seeing nitrates from these soils washing into rivers.

SAQ 3.7

Suggest why grassland which is grazed by animals accumulates larger amounts of nitrate in the soil than does grassland which is cut to make silage or hay.

Another cause of increasing quantities of leached nitrates is fixed nitrogen entering the soil from the air. In southern Britain, about $50\,kg\,ha^{-1}\,year^{-1}$ of nitrogen is added to the soil in this way. Some of this is from natural sources such as lightning, some as gaseous ammonia from urine from farm animals, and some from nitrogen oxides from car exhausts and power stations.

Problems caused by excess nitrates in fresh water

The concerns about high levels of nitrate in fresh water fall into two categories: threats to human health and damage to aquatic ecosystems.

Health threats

High levels of nitrate in the diet, especially in drinking water, have been linked to two possible human health problems. These are not caused by nitrate directly, but by nitrite, which is produced by the reduction of nitrate by bacteria in the stomach.

The first is called 'blue baby syndrome'. This can occur in bottle-fed babies up to 6 months old, if their feed is made up using water containing very high nitrate concentrations. The nitrite affects their haemoglobin, preventing the blood from carrying oxygen effectively. Severe cases are fatal. However, this problem has been exaggerated; there have only ever been 10 cases reported in Britain, and none at all in recent years.

The second is a possibility of an increased risk of stomach cancer. However, the evidence for this is very limited. Also the rates of stomach cancer in Britain have been falling steadily for many years, despite the rise in nitrate levels.

Nevertheless, no-one has ever shown that high levels of nitrate in drinking water are good for you, and it is probably wise to assume that they are not. Both the World Health Organisation and the European Union have set a limit of $50\,mg\,dm^{-3}$ for the maximum concentration of nitrate that should be allowed in drinking water.

Damage to aquatic ecosystems

High nitrate levels increase the growth of aquatic algae and plants. (High phosphate levels, produced by phosphates entering water in untreated sewage and waste from some industrial processes, also cause this to happen.) The rapid algal growth produces green murky water, and prevents light reaching plants growing on or near the bottom of the river or lake. These plants die and are decomposed by bacteria, whose populations rapidly increase. The bacteria respire, removing dissolved oxygen from the water. Organisms which require high levels of oxygen, such as most fish, and many nonvertebrates such as dragonfly larvae, must leave or die.

The rate at which dissolved oxygen is removed from water is known as the **biochemical oxygen demand**, or BOD. A high BOD is an indication of organic pollution.

The sequence of events described above is called **eutrophication**. Eutrophication generally decreases species diversity. Most people also find eutrophic rivers and lakes, which tend to be murky, less attractive than clear unpolluted ones.

Problems caused by excess nitrates on land

On agricultural land, the increasing use of fertilisers, especially ammonium nitrate, has reduced species diversity on grassland. Meadows containing a high diversity of flowering plants *(figure 3.16)* have become increasingly rare. Fertilisers increase the growth of grasses and plants such as nettles and docks. These grow so vigorously that they shade out smaller plants such as orchids. The loss of these species has been speeded up by the use of selective herbicides, which kill most plants other than grasses.

Ammonium nitrate can also break down to form ammonia, which is released into the air. There has been an estimated 50% increase in ammonia emission over Europe since 1950. Although most of this has probably come from animal waste as a result of intensive pig, poultry and cattle rearing systems, some has come from fertilisers. The ammonia in the air increases the rate at which sulphate is deposited, so increasing soil acidity. Acidification of soils is a major cause of damage to

forests in many parts of the northern hemisphere. You can read more about this in *Ecology and Conservation* in this series.

Measures to reduce problems caused by excess nitrates in soil and water

Plant growth, and therefore production of food, is often limited by lack of nitrates in the soil. Nitrogen shortage in wheat, for example, reduces the amount of RuBISCO (page 9), so reducing the rate of photosynthesis. By adding nitrogen-containing fertilisers, farmers increase production. A long-term experiment in which sugar beet was grown on two plots, one with added nitrogen and one with no fertiliser, showed that the yield from the unfertilised plot fell by 60% over 25 years.

The use of ammonium nitrate and other inorganic nitrogen-containing fertilisers has meant that more people can be fed more cheaply. We cannot do without nitrogen-containing fertilisers. However, farmers and conservationists now realise that inorganic fertilisers, and also organic fertilisers such as manure and slurry, must be used with care.

The long half-life of nitrates in the soil, and the relatively small contribution made by inorganic fertilisers to the amount of leached nitrate in ground water and rivers, means that simply reducing fertiliser inputs now is unlikely to have any immediate effect on nitrate levels in water. However, it is generally agreed that we should do our best to make sure that we do not make matters worse. The removal of nitrates from drinking water is a very expensive process. If we are to meet the standard of no more than 50 mg of nitrate per cubic decimetre, we must do what we can to cut down inputs of yet more nitrate into ground and river water.

The Ministry of Agriculture, Fisheries and Foods produces guidelines for farmers to help them to make sure that they do not increase

● *Figure 3.16* Hay meadows with a high diversity of species are now very rare. To create such a meadow, the fertility of the soil must be kept very low, to give the more attractive flowering plants a chance to compete with grasses, which grow vigorously when nitrates and phosphates are in plentiful supply.

the risk of high levels of nitrates being leached into fresh water. Most farmers are very willing to follow these guidelines. They have no wish to pollute water. Nor do they want to spend money on expensive fertilisers which are simply going to be washed away. These guidelines include the following recommendations:

■ avoid ploughing up old grassland;
■ do not apply excessive amounts of organic manures, as these are even more likely to produce large quantities of leached nitrates than are inorganic fertilisers;
■ leave a strip at least 10 metres wide next to water courses, where you do not spread animal wastes;

■ before applying inorganic fertilisers, measure the amount of nitrate in the soil, and calculate the probable needs of the crop to be grown, then apply just the right amount of fertiliser;
■ apply any fertiliser, whether inorganic or organic, at a time when the crop is actively growing, so that the plants will remove the nitrate from the soil before it can be leached: it is best to apply fertilisers in spring rather than autumn;
■ try not to leave land bare for any length of time, especially over winter, because nitrates are more easily leached from land with no plants growing on it.

SUMMARY

■ Energy flows through ecosystems. All energy enters an ecosystem as sunlight, and is converted to chemical energy in organic molecules during photosynthesis in producers. Energy is transferred along food chains as one organism feeds on another. Energy is lost at each transfer within and between organisms, mostly as heat produced during respiration. This results in a decrease in biomass and energy in successive trophic levels, which can be shown graphically by pyramids of biomass and energy respectively.

■ Matter cycles around ecosystems. Carbon dioxide from the air is fixed during photosynthesis, becoming part of organic molecules in plants. It is then passed from one organism to another as they feed on each other. Respiration, which occurs in all organisms, returns carbon dioxide to the air. Decomposers play a very important role in this cycling. Partially decayed plants and micro-organisms may accumulate underground to form fossil fuels, which hold large amounts of carbon. This is released as carbon dioxide during combustion.

■ Increasing rates of combustion of fossil fuels are increasing the amount of carbon dioxide in the air, which may cause global warming. Deforestation is also contributing to this effect. International agreements have been made to try to limit the amounts of carbon dioxide emitted to the atmosphere.

■ Nitrogen from the air is fixed by bacteria, some of which live freely in the soil and some, especially *Rhizobium*, which live in root nodules of leguminous plants. Fixed nitrogen, in the form of nitrates, is taken up by plants and used to synthesise amino acids and proteins, on which animals feed. Decomposers convert dead organisms and their waste products to ammonia, which is then converted to nitrite and nitrate by nitrifying bacteria. Denitrifying bacteria complete the cycle, converting inorganic nitrogen compounds to nitrogen gas.

■ There is concern about health and environmental problems caused by high levels of nitrates in water, which are partly caused by modern agricultural practices. Without the use of inorganic or organic fertilisers, food would be very much more expensive to produce. Guidelines have been produced to help farmers to understand how to minimise the risks of nitrate leaching from soil.

Questions

1 'Energy flows through an ecosystem, but matter cycles around it'. Discuss this statement, with reference to an ecosystem with which you are familiar.

2 Why are large carnivores rare?

3 Discuss the possible causes and effects of global warming. What should we be doing about this threat?

4 Two possible approaches to reducing the adverse effects of agriculture on the environment are:

- to farm very intensively on some areas of land, thus maximising rates of production on these areas and freeing other areas for conservation;

- to farm 'organically', using low inputs of fertilisers and pesticides.

Discuss the relative merits of these two approaches. Try to consider various points of view, such as those of farmers, conservationists and people buying food in shops. Do not forget that one person may be all of these people at once!

Genetic control of development

The structure of DNA and RNA

DNA stands for **deoxyribonucleic acid** and RNA for **ribonucleic acid**. DNA and RNA, like proteins and polysaccharides, are **macromolecules**. They are also **polymers**, made up of many similar, smaller molecules joined into a long chain. The smaller molecules from which DNA and RNA molecules are made are **nucleotides**. DNA and RNA are therefore **polynucleotides**.

Nucleotides

Figure 4.1 shows the structure of nucleotides. Nucleotides are made up of three smaller components. These are:

■ a phosphate group;
■ a nitrogen-containing base;
■ a pentose sugar.

There are five different nitrogen-containing bases found in DNA and RNA. In a DNA molecule they are **adenine, thymine, guanine** and **cytosine**. (Do not confuse adenine with adenosine which is part of the name of ATP – adenosine is adenine with a sugar joined to it; and don't confuse thymine with thiamine, which is a vitamin.) In an RNA molecule, the base thymine is never found. Instead, RNA molecules contain a base called **uracil**. These bases are often referred to by their first letters: **A, T, C, G** and **U.**

The pentose sugar can be either **ribose** (in RNA) or **deoxyribose** (in DNA). As their names suggest, deoxyribose is almost the same as ribose, except that it has one less oxygen atom in its molecule.

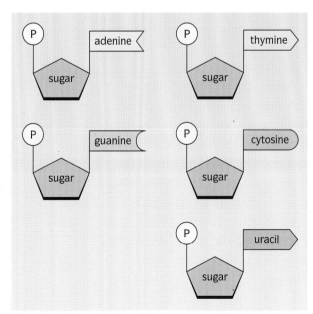

● **Figure 4.1** Nucleotides. A nucleotide is made of a phosphate group ⓟ, a 5-carbon sugar, and a nitrogen-containing base.

Figure 4.1 shows the five different nucleotides from which DNA and RNA molecules can be built up. *Figure 4.2* shows the structure of their components in more detail; you do not need to remember these structures, but if you enjoy biochemistry you may find them interesting.

Polynucleotides

To form the polynucleotides DNA and RNA, many nucleotides are linked together into a long chain. This takes place inside the nucleus, during interphase of the cell cycle.

Figure 4.3a shows the structure of part of a polynucleotide strand. It is formed of alternating sugars and phosphates linked together, with the bases projecting sideways.

RNA molecules are made of a single polynucleotide strand (*figure 4.4*). DNA molecules, however, are made of two polynucleotide strands lying side by side. The two strands are held together by **hydrogen bonds** between the bases (*figure 4.3b*).

From *figure 4.2*, you will see that the two purine bases, adenine and guanine, are larger molecules than the two pyrimidines, cytosine and thymine. In a DNA molecule, there is just enough room between the two sugar–phosphate back-bones for one purine and one pyrimidine molecule, so a purine in one strand must always be opposite a pyrimidine in the other. In fact, the pairing of the bases is even more precise than this. Adenine always pairs with thymine, while cytosine always

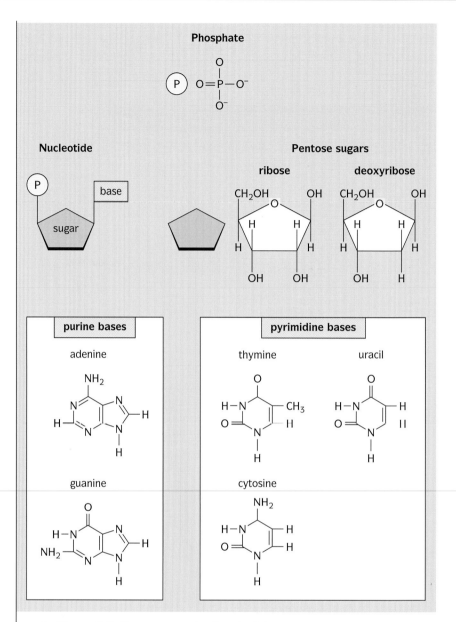

● *Figure 4.2* The components of nucleotides.

pairs with guanine: **A** with **T**, **C** with **G**. This **complementary base pairing** is a very important feature of polynucleotides, as you will see later.

The hydrogen bonds linking the bases, and therefore holding the two strands together, can be broken relatively easily. This happens during DNA replication and also during protein synthesis. Like complementary base pairing, this is a very important feature of the DNA molecule, which enables it to perform its role in its functions in the cell.

SAQ 4.1

Summarise the differences between the structures of DNA and RNA.

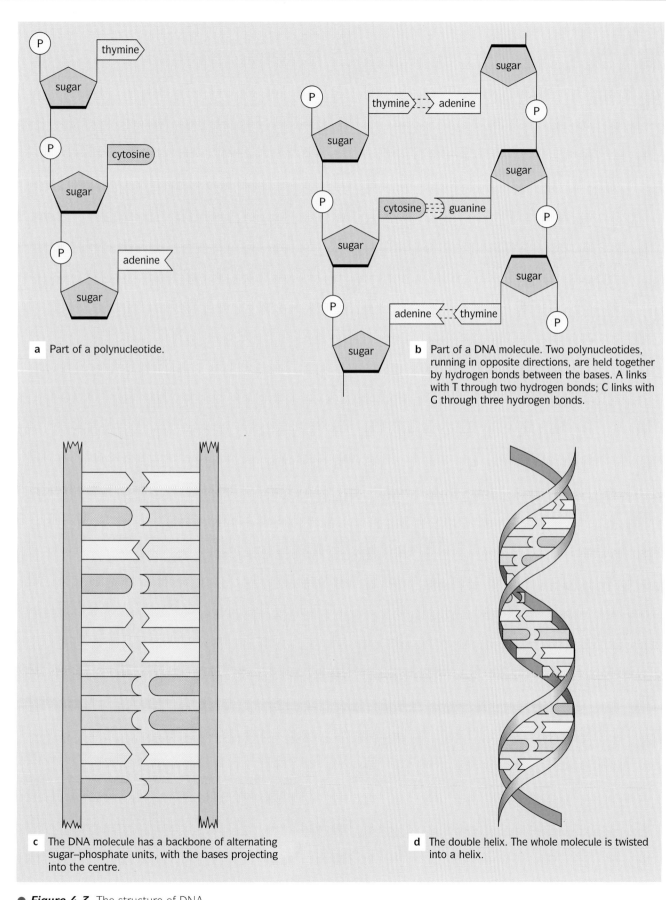

a Part of a polynucleotide.

b Part of a DNA molecule. Two polynucleotides, running in opposite directions, are held together by hydrogen bonds between the bases. A links with T through two hydrogen bonds; C links with G through three hydrogen bonds.

c The DNA molecule has a backbone of alternating sugar–phosphate units, with the bases projecting into the centre.

d The double helix. The whole molecule is twisted into a helix.

● *Figure 4.3* The structure of DNA.

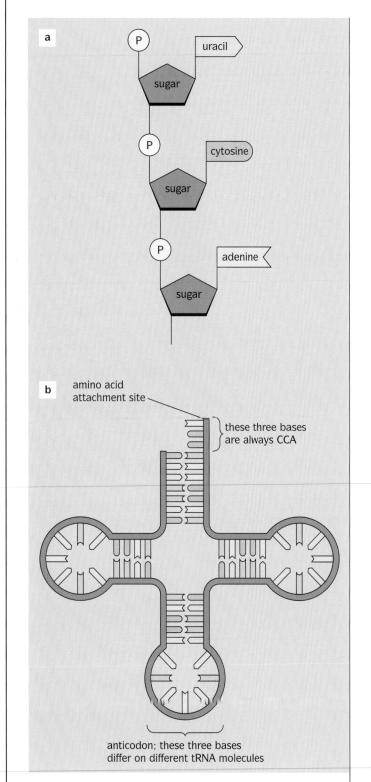

a

uracil

sugar

P

cytosine

sugar

P

adenine

sugar

P

b

amino acid
attachment site

these three bases
are always CCA

anticodon; these three bases
differ on different tRNA molecules

● *Figure 4.4* RNA.

a Part of a messenger RNA polynucleotide.

b Transfer RNA. The molecule is a single-stranded polynucleotide, folded into a clover-leaf shape. Transfer RNA
molecules with different anticodons are recognised by
different enzymes, which load them with their appropriate amino acid.

Box 4A Some other molecules containing nucleotides

DNA and RNA are not the only important biological
molecules which contain nucleotides. Three others
which you have met in this book are **ATP**, **NAD** and
NADP.

ATP is adenosine triphosphate. The structure of ATP
is shown in *figure 1.3*. It contains the base **adenine**
and the sugar **ribose**. A molecule made up of a base
and a sugar is called a **nucleoside**; in this case, the
nucleoside is **adenosine**.

ATP differs from the nucleotides in *figure 4.1* in that
it has *three* phosphate groups per molecule. However,
these phosphate groups can be lost, one by one, to
produce ADP and AMP (page 2). The structure of AMP
is shown in *figure 4.5*. You can see that this molecule
is identical to one of the nucleotides which are part of a
RNA molecule. So here are two molecules, RNA and
ATP, with very different functions, but with very similar
basic molecular structures.

NAD is nicotinamide adenine dinucleotide. Its structure is shown in *figure 4.6*. It is made of two
nucleotides linked together. In each nucleotide, the
sugar is ribose. In one nucleotide, the nitrogen-
containing base is adenine. In the other, there is something different – a group called a nicotinamide ring.
This is the reactive part of the molecule, which can
accept a hydrogen ion and two electrons. When it does
this, the molecule is reduced. These electrons can later
be released and donated to other molecules.

A slightly different form of NAD has a phosphate
group instead of the hydrogen on carbon 1 in the
ribose ring. This molecule is called NADP.

NAD and NADP play the role of hydrogen acceptor
in many metabolic reactions in all kinds of living organisms. You have seen how NAD does this in respiration
in chapter 2, and how NADP does it in photosynthesis
in chapter 1.

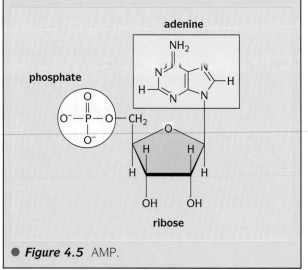

adenine

phosphate

ribose

● *Figure 4.5* AMP.

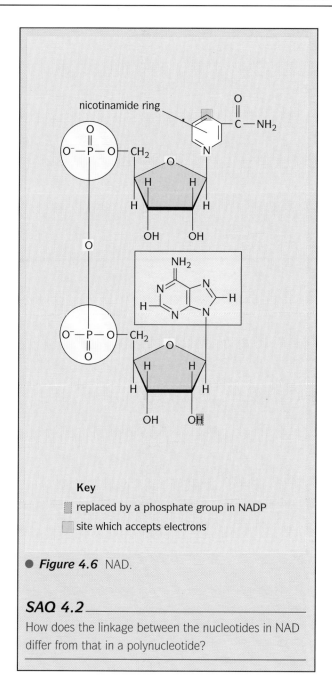

nicotinamide ring

Key

- replaced by a phosphate group in NADP
- site which accepts electrons

● *Figure 4.6* NAD.

SAQ 4.2

How does the linkage between the nucleotides in NAD differ from that in a polynucleotide?

DNA replication

The genetic molecule

If you were asked to design a molecule which could act as the genetic material in living things, where would you start?

One of the features of the 'genetic molecule' would have to be the ability to **carry instructions** – a sort of blueprint – for the construction and behaviour of cells, and the way in which they grow together to form a complete living organism. Another would be the **ability to be copied** perfectly, over and over again, so that whenever the nucleus of a cell divides it can pass on an exact copy of each 'genetic molecule' to the nuclei of each of its daughter cells.

Until 1944, biologists assumed that the 'genetic molecule' must be a protein. Only proteins were thought to be complex enough to be able to carry the huge number of instructions which would be necessary to make such a complicated structure as a living organism. But in 1944, three American scientists, Avery, Macleod and McCarty, proved beyond doubt that the 'genetic molecule' was not a protein at all, but DNA.

It was not until 1953 that James Watson and Francis Crick worked out the basic structure of the DNA molecule. To them, it was immediately obvious how this molecule could be copied perfectly, time and time again.

Watson and Crick suggested that the two strands of the DNA molecule could split apart. New nucleotides could then line up along each strand opposite their appropriate partners, and join up to form complementary strands along each half of the original molecule. The new DNA molecules would be just like the old ones, because each base would only pair with its complementary one. Each pair of strands could then wind up again into a double helix, exactly like the original one.

This idea proved to be correct. The process is shown in *figure 4.7*. This method of copying is called **semi-conservative replication**, because *half* of the original molecule is *kept* (conserved) in each of the new molecules.

SAQ 4.3

a What other types of molecules, apart from nucleotides, are needed for DNA replication to take place? (Use *figure 4.7* to help you to answer this.) What does each of these molecules do?

b In what part of a eukaryotic cell does DNA replication take place?

DNA replication takes place when a cell is not dividing. This is in interphase in eukaryotic cells.

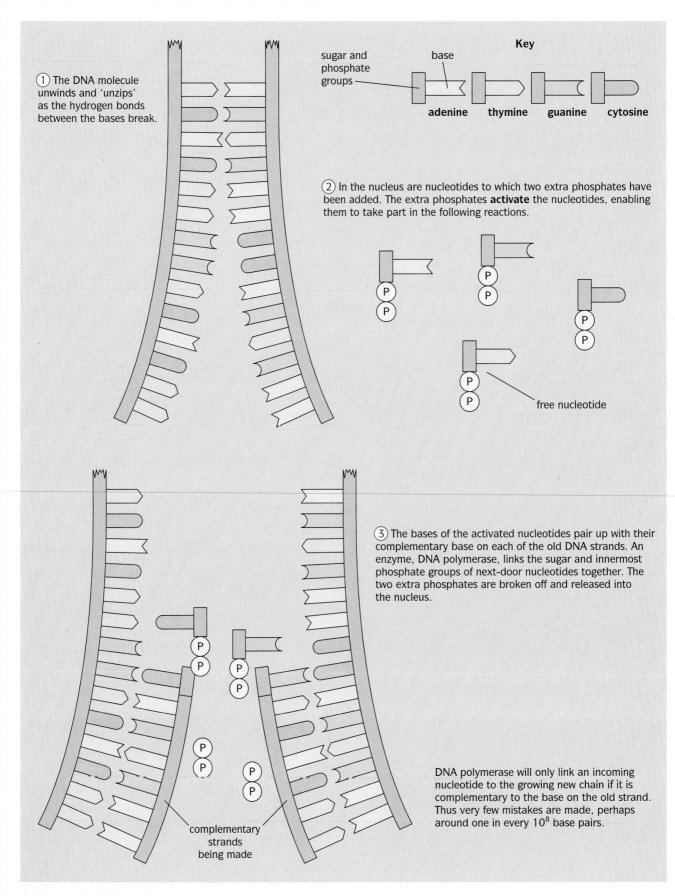

① The DNA molecule unwinds and 'unzips' as the hydrogen bonds between the bases break.

Key

sugar and phosphate groups

base

adenine **thymine** **guanine** **cytosine**

② In the nucleus are nucleotides to which two extra phosphates have been added. The extra phosphates **activate** the nucleotides, enabling them to take part in the following reactions.

free nucleotide

③ The bases of the activated nucleotides pair up with their complementary base on each of the old DNA strands. An enzyme, DNA polymerase, links the sugar and innermost phosphate groups of next-door nucleotides together. The two extra phosphates are broken off and released into the nucleus.

DNA polymerase will only link an incoming nucleotide to the growing new chain if it is complementary to the base on the old strand. Thus very few mistakes are made, perhaps around one in every 10^8 base pairs.

complementary strands being made

● **Figure 4.7** DNA replication.

DNA, RNA and protein synthesis

DNA controls protein synthesis

How can a single type of molecule like DNA control all the activities of a cell? The answer is very logical. All chemical reactions in cells, and therefore all their activities, are controlled by enzymes (described in *Foundation Biology* in this series). Enzymes are proteins. DNA is a code for polypeptides and proteins and therefore controls which proteins are made. Thus DNA controls the cell's activities.

Protein molecules are made up of strings of amino acids. The shape and behaviour of a protein molecule depends on the exact sequence of these amino acids, that is its primary structure. DNA controls protein structure by determining the exact order in which the amino acids join together when proteins are made in a cell.

The triplet code

The sequence of bases or nucleotides in a DNA molecule is a code for the sequence of amino acids in a polypeptide. *Figure 4.8* shows a very short length of a DNA molecule, just enough to code for four amino acids. The code is carried in the base sequence of only one of the two strands of the DNA molecule. In this case, assume that this is the strand on the left of the diagram.

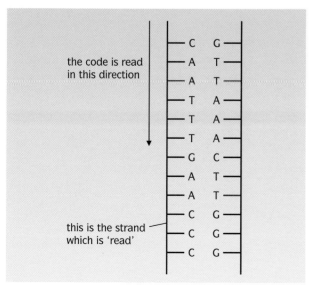

● **Figure 4.8** A length of DNA coding for four amino acids.

The code is a three-letter, or **triplet**, code. Each sequence of three bases stands for one amino acid. The sequence is always read in one particular direction. Reading from the top of the left-hand strand, the code is:

CAA   which stands for the amino acid valine
TTT   which stands for the amino acid lysine
GAA   which stands for the amino acid leucine
CCC   which stands for the amino acid glycine

So this short piece of DNA carries the instruction to the cell: 'Make a chain of amino acids in the sequence valine, lysine, leucine and glycine'.

SAQ 4.4

There are 20 different amino acids which cells use for making proteins.

a How many different amino acids could the triplet code code for? (Remember that there are four possible bases, and that the code is always read in just one direction on the DNA strand.)

b Suggest how the 'spare' triplets might be used.

c Explain why the code could not be a two-letter code.

The complete set of codes is shown on page 82.

Genes and genomes

DNA molecules can be enormous. The bacterium *E. coli* has just one DNA molecule which is four million base pairs long. There is enough information here to code for several thousand proteins. The total DNA of a human cell is estimated to be about 3×10^9 base pairs long. However, it is thought that only 3% of this DNA actually codes for protein, the function of the remainder being uncertain.

A part of a DNA molecule which codes for just one polypeptide is called a **gene**. One DNA molecule contains many genes. In humans, it is estimated that there are about 100 000 genes.

The total set of genes in a cell is called the **genome**. The genome is the total information in one cell. Since all cells in the same individual contain the same information, the genome represents the genetic code of that organism.

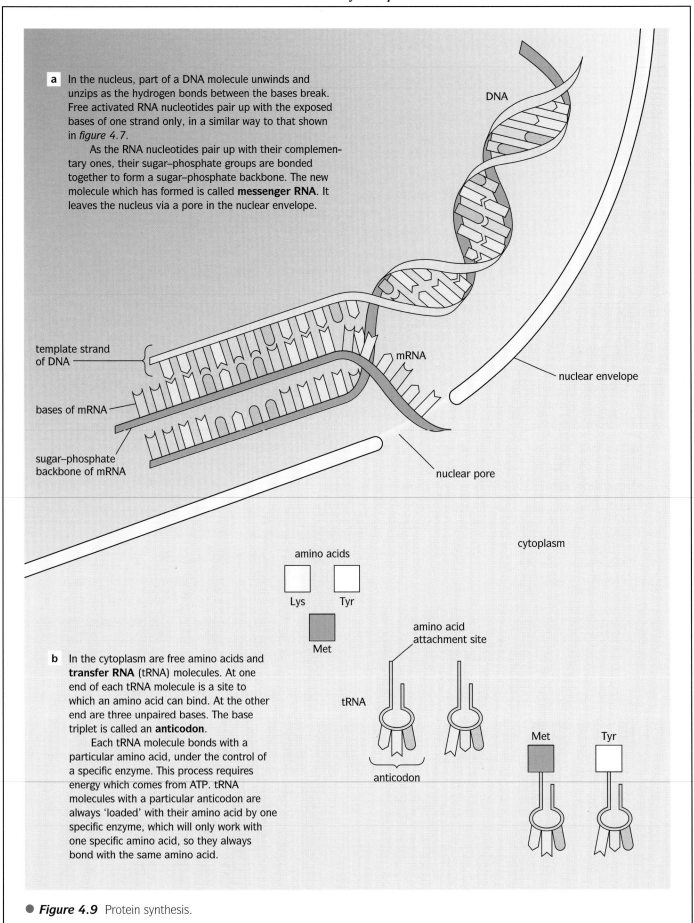

a In the nucleus, part of a DNA molecule unwinds and unzips as the hydrogen bonds between the bases break. Free activated RNA nucleotides pair up with the exposed bases of one strand only, in a similar way to that shown in *figure 4.7*.

As the RNA nucleotides pair up with their complementary ones, their sugar–phosphate groups are bonded together to form a sugar–phosphate backbone. The new molecule which has formed is called **messenger RNA**. It leaves the nucleus via a pore in the nuclear envelope.

DNA

template strand of DNA

bases of mRNA

sugar–phosphate backbone of mRNA

mRNA

nuclear envelope

nuclear pore

cytoplasm

amino acids

Lys   Tyr

Met

amino acid attachment site

tRNA

anticodon

Met   Tyr

b In the cytoplasm are free amino acids and **transfer RNA** (tRNA) molecules. At one end of each tRNA molecule is a site to which an amino acid can bind. At the other end are three unpaired bases. The base triplet is called an **anticodon**.

Each tRNA molecule bonds with a particular amino acid, under the control of a specific enzyme. This process requires energy which comes from ATP. tRNA molecules with a particular anticodon are always 'loaded' with their amino acid by one specific enzyme, which will only work with one specific amino acid, so they always bond with the same amino acid.

● *Figure 4.9* Protein synthesis.

c Meanwhile, also in the cytoplasm, the mRNA molecule attaches to a ribosome. Ribosomes are made of ribosomal RNA (rRNA) and protein and contain a small and a large subunit. The mRNA binds to the small subunit. Six bases at a time are exposed to the large subunit.

 The first three exposed bases, or **codon**, are always AUG. A tRNA molecule with the complementary anticodon, UAC, forms hydrogen bonds with this codon. This tRNA molecule has the amino acid methionine attached to it.

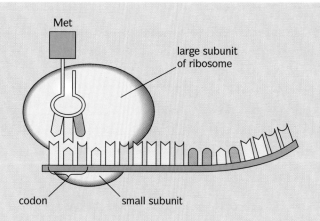

d A second tRNA molecule bonds with the next three exposed bases. This one brings a different amino acid. The two amino acids are held closely together, and a peptide bond is formed between them. This reaction is catalysed by the enzyme peptidyl transferase, which is found in the small subunit of the ribosome.

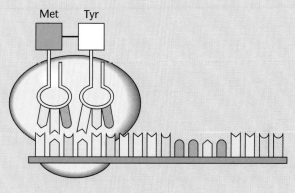

e The ribosome now moves along the mRNA, exposing the next three bases on the ribosome. A third tRNA molecule brings a third amino acid, which joins to the second one. The first tRNA leaves.

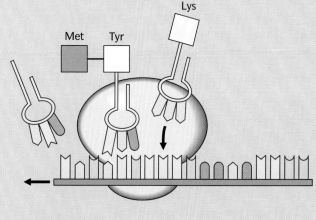

f The polypeptide chain continues to grow, until a 'stop' codon is exposed on the ribosome. This is UAA, UAC or UGA.

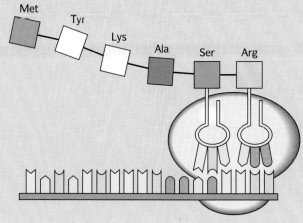

● **Figure 4.9** (cont.)

Protein synthesis

The code on the DNA molecule is used to determine how the polypeptide molecule is constructed. *Figure 4.9* describes the process in detail, but briefly the process is as follows.

In the nucleus, a complementary copy of the code from a gene is made by building a molecule of a different type of nucleic acid, called **messenger RNA (mRNA)**, using one strand of the DNA as a template.

The mRNA leaves the nucleus, and attaches to a **ribosome**.

In the cytoplasm there are molecules of **transfer RNA (tRNA)**. These have a triplet of bases at one end and a region where an amino acid can attach at the other. There are at least 20 different sorts of tRNA molecules, each with a particular triplet of bases at one end and able to attach to a specific amino acid at the other.

The tRNA molecules pick up their specific amino acids from the cytoplasm and bring them to the mRNA on the ribosome. The triplet of bases (an **anticodon**) of each tRNA links up with a complementary triplet (a **codon**) on the mRNA molecule. Two tRNA molecules fit onto the ribosome at any one time. This brings two amino acids side by side and peptide bonds are formed between them.

So the base sequence on the DNA molecule determines the base sequence on the mRNA, which determines which tRNA molecules can link up with them. Since each type of tRNA molecule is specific for just one amino acid, this determines the sequence in which the amino acids are linked together as the polypeptide molecule is made.

The first stage in this process, that is the making of a mRNA molecule which carries a complementary copy of the code from part of the DNA molecule, is called **transcription**, because this is when the DNA code is **transcribed**, or copied, on to an mRNA molecule. The last stage is called **translation**, because this is when the DNA code is **translated** into an amino acid sequence.

SAQ 4.5

Draw a simple flow diagram to illustrate the important stages in protein synthesis.

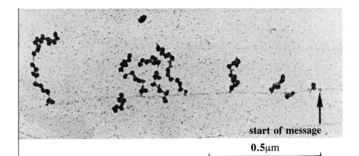

start of message

0.5μm

● **Figure 4.10** Protein synthesis in a bacterium. In bacteria, there is no nucleus, so protein synthesis can begin as soon as some mRNA has been made. Here, the long thread running from left to right is DNA. Nine mRNA molecules are being made, using this DNA as a template. Each mRNA molecule is immediately being read by ribosomes, which you can see as black blobs attached along the mRNAs. The mRNA strand at the left hand end is much longer than the one at the right, indicating that the mRNA is being synthesised working along the DNA molecule from right to left.

Sickle cell anaemia

In theory, if we know enough about the DNA in a cell, we should be able to predict what that cell will be like. But we cannot yet do this with even the simplest cells, such as bacteria. Even if we know the complete sequences of bases in all the DNA in a cell, we still do not know which parts of the DNA will be active in producing mRNA, and therefore which proteins will be made and when. We still do not know just what all these proteins will do, and when they will do it. The complexities are too great, even with a simple cell.

However, we do have quite a good understanding of some small parts of this giant puzzle, and some of the parts which we already understand are about the DNA and proteins in *human* cells. One of these is the way in which the disease sickle cell anaemia is caused.

Haemoglobin is the red pigment in red blood cells which carries oxygen around the body. A haemoglobin molecule is made up of four polypeptide chains, each with one iron-containing haem group in the centre. Two of these polypeptide chains are called α chains, and the other two β chains. (The structure of haemoglobin is described in *Foundation Biology*, in this series.)

The gene which codes for the amino acid sequence in the β chains is not the same in everyone. In most people, the β chains begin with the amino acid sequence:

Val – His – Leu – Thr – Pro – Glu – Glu – Lys –

But in some people, the chain begins:

Val – His – Leu – Thr – Pro – Val – Glu – Lys –

SAQ 4.6

The base sequence in the gene coding for these two different amino acid sequences differs by just one base. What is it? (You will need to look up the genetic code on page 82.)

This small difference in the amino acid sequence makes little difference to the haemoglobin molecule when it is combined with oxygen. But when it is not combined with oxygen, the 'unusual' β chains make the haemoglobin molecule much less soluble. The molecules tend to stick to each other, forming long fibres inside the red blood cells. The red cells are pulled out of shape, into a half-moon or sickle shape. When this happens, the distorted cells become quite useless at transporting oxygen. They also get stuck in small capillaries, stopping any unaffected cells from getting through *(figure 4.11)*.

A person with these unusual β chains can suffer severe anaemia (lack of oxygen transported to the cells) and may die. It is especially common in some parts of Africa, and in India. You can read about the reasons for this distribution on pages 75–6.

Phenylketonuria

Phenylketonuria, or **PKU**, is another disease caused by an abnormal base sequence in part of a DNA molecule. However, in PKU the affected gene codes for an enzyme, not for an oxygen-carrying pigment.

The enzyme affected in PKU is phenylalanine hydroxylase. People with the disease lack this enzyme because their DNA does not carry the correct code for making it. Phenylalanine hydroxylase helps to catalyse the conversion of the amino acid phenylalanine to tyrosine, which can then be converted into melanin.

$$\text{phenylalanine} \xrightarrow{\text{phenylalanine hydroxylase}} \text{tyrosine} \longrightarrow \text{melanin}$$

Phenylalanine is found in many different kinds of foods. Melanin is the brown pigment in skin and hair. If phenylalanine cannot be converted to tyrosine, then little melanin is formed, so people with PKU frequently have a lighter skin and hair colour than normal.

However, a far more important problem which arises is that phenylalanine accumulates in the blood and tissue fluid. This causes severe

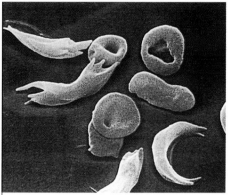

● **Figure 4.11** A scanning electron micrograph of red blood cells from a person with sickle cell anaemia. You can see both normal and sickled cells.

brain damage in young children. Children with untreated PKU become severely mentally retarded.

All babies born in the UK are tested for PKU at birth, simply by testing the phenylalanine levels in their blood. This testing is very important because brain damage can be completely prevented if a child with PKU is, at birth, put on to a diet which does not contain phenylalanine.

Mutations

A mutation is an unpredictable change in the genetic make-up of a cell. Mutations may affect the sequence of bases in a DNA molecule, in which case they are known as **gene mutations**. Alternatively, they may affect the structure or numbers of chromosomes in a cell, in which case they are known as **chromosome mutations**.

Both sickle cell anaemia and PKU are caused by 'incorrect' base sequences in part of a DNA molecule. These 'incorrect' base sequences have arisen from the 'correct' ones by mutation, that is they are gene mutations. The mutation may have occurred many generations back, in a cell in an ovary or testis which developed into an egg or sperm and was then passed on from parents to children.

Some of the causes and effects of mutations are described in *Foundation Biology* in this series.

Genetic engineering

The structure of DNA, and the way in which it codes for protein synthesis, was worked out during the 1950s and 1960s. Since then, this knowledge has developed to the level at which we can change the DNA in a cell, and so change the proteins which that cell synthesises. This is called **genetic engineering**.

Insulin production

To explain the principles of genetic engineering, we will look at one example, that is the use of genetically engineered bacteria to mass-produce human insulin.

One form of diabetes mellitus is caused by the inability of the β cells in the pancreas to produce insulin. (You can read more about this in *Foundation Biology*.) People with this disease need regular injections of insulin which, until recently, was extracted from the pancreases of pigs or cattle. This extraction was expensive, and many people did not like the idea of using insulin from an animal. Moreover, insulin from pigs or cattle is not identical to human insulin.

In the 1970s, biotechnology companies began to work on the idea of inserting the gene for human insulin into a bacterium, and then using this bacterium to make insulin. They tried several different approaches, finally succeeding in the early 1980s.

The procedure had several stages as described below and shown in *figure 4.12*.

Isolating the insulin gene

Insulin is a small protein. The first task was to isolate the gene coding for human insulin from all the rest of the DNA in a human cell. In this

instance, there were problems in doing this directly. Instead, **mRNA** carrying the code for making insulin was extracted from β cells from a human pancreas.

The mRNA was then incubated with an enzyme called **reverse transcriptase** which comes from a special group of viruses called retroviruses. This enzyme does something which does not normally happen in human cells – it causes DNA to be made from RNA. Complementary DNA molecules were formed from the mRNA from the pancreas cells. First, single-stranded molecules were formed, which were then converted to double-stranded DNA. These DNA molecules carried the code for making insulin; that is, they were insulin genes.

In order to enable these insulin genes to be able to stick onto other DNA at a later stage in the procedure, they were given 'sticky ends'. This was done by adding lengths of single-stranded DNA made up of guanine nucleotides to each end, using enzymes.

Inserting the gene into a vector

In order to get the human insulin gene into a bacterium a go-between, called a **vector**, has to be used. The vectors used in genetic engineering are **viruses** and **plasmids**.

A plasmid is a small, circular piece of DNA which can be found in many bacteria. Plasmids are able to insert themselves into bacteria so, if you can put your piece of human DNA into a plasmid, the plasmid can put it into a bacterium. Viruses can act in a similar way to plasmids.

To get the plasmids, the bacteria containing them were treated with enzymes to dissolve their cell walls. These were then centrifuged, so that the relatively large bacterial chromosomes were separated from the much smaller plasmids. The circular DNA molecule making up the plasmid was then cut open using an enzyme. Once again, sticky ends were added, but this time the nucleotides used to make these single strands contained cytosine.

The cut plasmid and the cut human DNA were mixed together, and the C and G bases on their sticky ends paired together. The nucleotide backbones were linked using an enzyme called **DNA ligase**, so that the human insulin gene became part of the plasmid.

Isolation of human gene

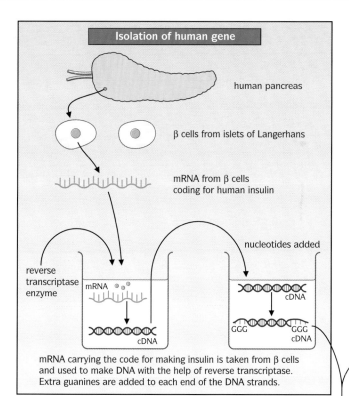

human pancreas

β cells from islets of Langerhans

mRNA from β cells coding for human insulin

nucleotides added

reverse transcriptase enzyme

mRNA carrying the code for making insulin is taken from β cells and used to make DNA with the help of reverse transcriptase. Extra guanines are added to each end of the DNA strands.

Preparation of vector

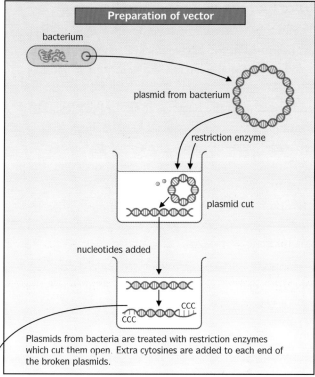

bacterium

plasmid from bacterium

restriction enzyme

plasmid cut

nucleotides added

Plasmids from bacteria are treated with restriction enzymes which cut them open. Extra cytosines are added to each end of the broken plasmids.

Formation of recombinant DNA

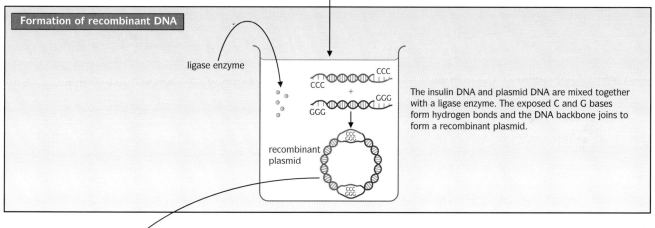

ligase enzyme

recombinant plasmid

The insulin DNA and plasmid DNA are mixed together with a ligase enzyme. The exposed C and G bases form hydrogen bonds and the DNA backbone joins to form a recombinant plasmid.

Manufacture

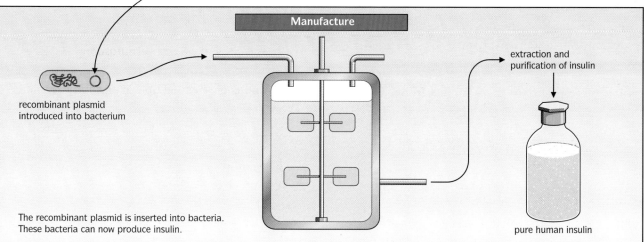

extraction and purification of insulin

recombinant plasmid introduced into bacterium

The recombinant plasmid is inserted into bacteria. These bacteria can now produce insulin.

pure human insulin

● *Figure 4.12* Producing insulin from genetically engineered bacteria.

Inserting the gene into the bacteria

The plasmids were now mixed with bacteria. In the case of insulin, the bacterium was *Escherichia coli*, a common, usually harmless, bacterium which lives in the human alimentary canal. A small proportion, perhaps 1%, of the bacteria took up the plasmids containing the insulin gene. These bacteria were separated from the others using another gene, for antibiotic resistance, which was introduced at the same time as the human insulin gene. When the bacteria were treated with antibiotic, only the ones containing the resistance gene (and therefore the insulin gene) survived.

The genetically engineered bacteria are now cultured on a large scale. They secrete insulin, which is extracted, purified and sold for use by people with diabetes.

Other uses of genetic engineering

Insulin production was one of the earliest success stories for genetic engineering. Since then, there have been many others. Other human protein hormones have been synthesised, for example human growth hormone. Enzymes are made, for use in the food industry, for example, or in biological washing powders.

Genetic engineering can introduce genes into any organism, not just bacteria. Recent developments give hope for the success of **gene therapy** in humans, in which 'good' copies of genes are inserted into cells of people with 'defective' ones. This could be used to treat genetic diseases, such as cystic fibrosis. However, at the moment there are problems in getting the genes into enough cells for there to be any useful effect.

Genes can be inserted into plants, too. Genes conferring resistance to pests can be extracted from a wild plant and inserted into a crop plant, for example.

You can read much more about these processes, and about some of the potential problems associated with them, in the books *Microbiology and Biotechnology* and *Applications of Genetics* in this series.

SUMMARY

- DNA and RNA are polynucleotides, made up of long chains of nucleotides. A nucleotide contains a pentose sugar, a phosphate group and a nitrogen-containing base. A DNA molecule consists of two polynucleotide chains, linked by hydrogen bonds between bases. Adenine always pairs with thymine, and cytosine with guanine. RNA, which comes in several different forms, has only one polynucleotide chain, although this may be twisted back on itself, as in tRNA. In RNA, the base thymine is replaced by uracil.

- DNA molecules replicate during interphase. The hydrogen bonds between the bases break, allowing free nucleotides to fall into position opposite their complementary ones on each strand of the original DNA molecule. Adjacent nucleotides are then linked, through their phosphates and sugars, to form new strands. Two complete new molecules are thus formed from one old one, each new molecule containing one old strand and one new.

- The sequence of bases (or nucleotides) on a DNA molecule codes for the sequence of amino acids in a protein (or polypeptide). Each amino acid is coded for by three bases. A length of DNA coding for one complete protein or polypeptide is a gene.

- During protein synthesis, a complementary copy of the base sequence on a gene is made, by building a molecule of mRNA against one DNA strand. The mRNA then moves to a ribosome in the cytoplasm. tRNA molecules with complementary triplets of bases temporarily pair with the base triplets on mRNA, bringing appropriate amino acids. As two amino acids are held side by side, a peptide bond forms between them. The ribosome moves along the mRNA molecule, so that appropriate amino acids are gradually linked together, following the sequence laid down by the base sequence on the mRNA.

- A small change in the base sequence of DNA can result in a change in the amino acid sequence of a protein which is made in the cell. This may affect the activity of the protein, as in the diseases sickle cell anaemia and phenylketonuria.

- DNA may be transferred from one species to another by means of genetic engineering.

Questions

1 Discuss the ways in which the structure of DNA allows it to carry out its functions.

2 Search recent newspapers and scientific magazines (for example *New Scientist*) for current examples of genetic engineering in the news. With reference to one or more such examples, discuss:

- your own feelings towards the potential usefulness and harm which may result from genetic engineering;

- the level of understanding of journalists and members of the public concerning the science behind these issues.

Chapter five

The passage of information from parent to offspring

By the end of this chapter you should be able to:

1 understand that cells of diploid organisms contain two copies of each gene, while haploid gametes contain only one copy of each gene;

2 explain the meanings of the terms *allele*, *homozygous*, *heterozygous*, *codominant*, *dominant*, *recessive*, *genotype* and *phenotype*;

3 choose and use suitable symbols for alleles of genes showing codominance or dominance;

4 draw genetic diagrams to explain the results of crosses in which one gene locus is considered (monohybrid crosses) and crosses in which two gene loci are considered (dihybrid crosses);

5 describe the use of test crosses in both monohybrid and dihybrid inheritance;

6 draw genetic diagrams to explain the results of crosses in which multiple alleles of a single gene are involved;

7 draw genetic diagrams to explain the results of crosses in which sex linkage is involved;

8 understand and describe examples showing how environment can interact with genes to affect phenotype.

Shortly before a cell divides by mitosis or meiosis, the DNA becomes visible as chromosomes. Each chromosome contains two identical DNA molecules, one in each **chromatid**. The DNA is associated with proteins.

In animals and many plants, there are two complete sets of chromosomes in each cell. These organisms are said to be **diploid**.

During sexual reproduction, DNA molecules are passed from the two parents to their offspring. Each offspring must receive one complete set of chromosomes from each parent – no more, no less. In this way, each offspring ends up with two complete sets of chromosomes, just like their parents.

In order to achieve this, cells called **gametes** are produced by each prospective parent. This is done by meiosis, which is described in *Foundation Biology*. Gametes have just a single set of chromosomes, that is they are **haploid** cells.

At fertilisation, gametes from two parents fuse together to form a cell called a **zygote**. The zygote contains one complete set of chromosomes from each gamete, that is two complete sets altogether, so the zygote is a diploid cell.

You will remember that a gene is a length of DNA which codes for the production of a polypeptide molecule. One chromosome contains enough DNA to code for many polypeptides.

Chromosomes that contain DNA for making the same polypeptides are said to be **homologous**. So, in a diploid cell, there are two copies of each gene. The two copies lie in the same position, or **locus**, on the two homologous chromosomes *(figure 5.1)*.

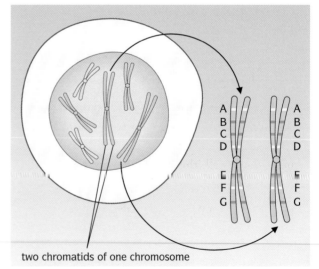

two chromatids of one chromosome

● *Figure 5.1* Homologous chromosomes carry the same genes at the same loci. Just seven genes, labelled A to G, are shown on these chromosomes, but there are often hundreds or thousands of genes on each chromosome. This is a diploid cell as there are two complete sets of chromosomes ($2n = 6$).

Alleles

The number of chromosomes per cell is characteristic for each species. Human cells contain 46 chromosomes, two each of 23 types. Each type is numbered and has its own particular genes. (They are shown in *figure 2.2* in *Foundation Biology*.) For example, the gene which codes for the production of the β polypeptide of the haemoglobin molecule is on chromosome 11. Each cell contains two copies of this gene, one maternal in origin (from the mother) and one paternal (from the father).

There are several forms or varieties of this gene. You have already met two of them, on page 51. One variety contains the base sequence CCTGAGGAG, and codes for the normal β polypeptide. Another variety contains the base sequence CCTGTGGAG, and codes for the sickle cell β polypeptide. These different varieties of the same gene are called **alleles**.

Genotype

Most genes, including the β polypeptide gene, have several different alleles. For the moment, we will consider only these two alleles of the β polypeptide gene.

To make life easier, the different alleles of a gene can be represented by symbols. In this case, they can be represented as follows:

H^N = the allele for the normal β polypeptide
H^S = the allele for the sickle cell β polypeptide

The letter H stands for the locus of the haemoglobin gene, while the superscripts N and S stand for particular alleles of the gene.

In a human cell, there are two copies of the β polypeptide gene. The two copies might be:

$H^N H^N$ or $H^S H^S$ or $H^N H^S$.

The alleles that a person has form their **genotype**. In this case, where we are considering just two different alleles, there are three possible genotypes.

SAQ 5.1

If there were three different alleles, how many possible genotypes would there be?

A genotype in which the two alleles of a gene are the same, for example $H^N H^N$, is said to be **homozygous** for that particular gene. A genotype in which the two alleles of a gene are different, for example $H^N H^S$, is said to be **heterozygous** for that gene. The organism can also be described as homozygous or heterozygous for that characteristic.

SAQ 5.2

How many of the genotypes in your answer to question 5.1 are homozygous, and how many are heterozygous?

Genotype affects phenotype

A person with the genotype $H^N H^N$ has two copies of the gene in each cell coding for the production of the normal β polypeptide. All of their haemoglobin will be normal.

A person with the genotype $H^S H^S$ has two copies of the gene in each cell coding for the production of the sickle cell β polypeptide. All of their haemoglobin will be sickle cell haemoglobin. The person will have sickle cell disease. As you have seen, this is a very dangerous disease, in which great care has to be taken not to allow the blood to become short of oxygen, or death may occur.

A person with the genotype $H^N H^S$ has one allele of the haemoglobin gene in each cell coding for the production of the normal β polypeptide, and one coding for the production of the sickle cell β polypeptide. Half of their haemoglobin will be normal, and half will be sickle cell haemoglobin. They will have sickle cell trait, and are sometimes referred to as carriers. They will probably be completely unaware of this, because they have enough normal haemoglobin to carry enough oxygen, and so will have no problems at all. They will appear to be perfectly normal. Difficulties arise only very occasionally, for example if a person with sickle cell trait does strenuous exercise at high altitudes, when oxgyen concentrations in the blood might become very low.

The observable characteristics of an individual are called their **phenotype**. We will normally use the word 'phenotype' to describe just the one or two particular characteristics that we are interested in. In this case, we are considering the characteristic of having, or not having, sickle cell anaemia.

Genotype	Phenotype
$H^N H^N$	normal
$H^N H^S$	normal, but with sickle cell trait
$H^S H^S$	sickle cell anaemia

● *Table 5.1*

Inheriting genes

In sexual reproduction, haploid gametes are made, following meiosis, from the nuclei of diploid body cells. Each gamete contains one of each pair of chromosomes. Therefore, each gamete contains only one copy of each gene.

Think about what will happen when sperms are made in the testes of a man who has the genotype $H^N H^S$. Each time a cell divides during meiosis, four gametes will be made, two of them with the H^N allele and two with the H^S allele. Of all the millions of sperms which are made in his lifetime, half will have the genotype H^N and half will have the genotype H^S *(figure 5.2)*. Similarly, a heterozygous woman will produce eggs of which half have the genotype H^N and half have the genotype H^S.

This information can be used to predict the possible genotypes of children born to a couple who are both heterozygous. Each time fertilisation occurs, either a H^N sperm or a H^S sperm may fertilise either a H^N egg or a H^S egg. The possible results can be shown like this.

		Genotypes of eggs	
		H^N	H^S
Genotypes of sperm	H^N	$H^N H^N$ normal	$H^N H^S$ sickle cell trait
	H^S	$H^N H^S$ sickle cell trait	$H^S H^S$ sickle cell anaemia

● *Figure 5.2* Meiosis of a heterozygous cell produces gametes of two different genotypes. Only one pair of homologous chromosomes is shown.

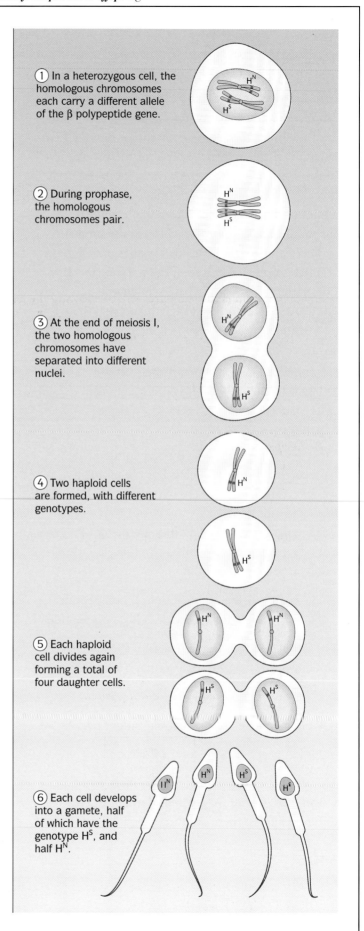

① In a heterozygous cell, the homologous chromosomes each carry a different allele of the β polypeptide gene.

② During prophase, the homologous chromosomes pair.

③ At the end of meiosis I, the two homologous chromosomes have separated into different nuclei.

④ Two haploid cells are formed, with different genotypes.

⑤ Each haploid cell divides again forming a total of four daughter cells.

⑥ Each cell develops into a gamete, half of which have the genotype H^S, and half H^N.

As there are equal numbers of each type of sperm and each type of egg, the chances of each of these four possibilities are also equal. Each time a child is conceived, there is a 1 in 4 chance that it will have the genotype $H^N H^N$, a 1 in 4 chance that it will be $H^S H^S$ and a 2 in 4 chance that it will be $H^N H^S$. Another way of describing these chances is to say that the probability of a child being $H^S H^S$ is 0.25, the probability of being $H^N H^N$ is 0.25, and the probability of being $H^N H^S$ is 0.5. It is important to realise that these are only *probabilities*. It would not be surprising if this couple had two children, both of whom had the genotype $H^S H^S$ and so suffered from sickle cell anaemia.

Genetic diagrams

A genetic diagram is the standard way of showing the genotypes of offspring which might be expected from two parents. To illustrate this, let us consider a different example, flower colour in snap-dragons (*Antirrhinum*).

One of the genes for flower colour has two alleles, namely C^R which gives red flowers, and C^W which gives white flowers. The phenotypes produced by each genotype are:

Genotype	Phenotype
$C^R C^R$	red
$C^R C^W$	pink
$C^W C^W$	white

What colour flowers would be expected in the offspring from a red and a pink snapdragon?

Parents' phenotypes	red	pink
Parents' genotypes	$C^R C^R$	$C^R C^W$
Genotypes of gametes	all C^R	C^R or C^W
		in equal proportions

Offspring genotypes and phenotypes

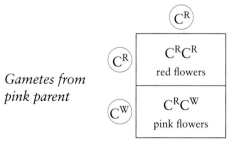

Thus, you would expect about half of the offspring to have red flowers and half to have pink flowers.

Dominance

In the examples used so far, both of the alleles in a heterozygous organism have an effect on the phenotype. A person with the genotype $H^N H^S$ has some normal haemoglobin and some sickle haemoglobin. A snapdragon with the genotype $C^R C^W$ has some red colour and some white colour, so that the flowers appear pink. Alleles which behave like this are said to be **codominant** alleles.

Frequently, however, only one allele has an effect in a heterozygous organism. This allele is said to be the **dominant** allele, while the one which has no effect is **recessive**. An example is stem colour in tomatoes. There are two alleles for stem colour, one of which produces green stems, and the other purple stems. In a tomato plant which has one allele for purple stems and one allele for green stems, the stems are exactly the same shade of purple as in a plant which has two alleles for purple stems. The allele for purple stems is dominant, and the allele for green stems is recessive.

When alleles of a gene behave like this, their symbols are written using a capital letter for the dominant allele and a small letter for the recessive allele. You are often free to choose the symbols you will use. In this case, the symbols could be **A** for the purple allele and **a** for the green allele. The possible genotypes and phenotypes for stem colour are:

Genotype	*Phenotype*
AA	purple stem
Aa	purple stem
aa	green stem

It is a good idea, when choosing symbols to use for alleles, to use letters where the capital looks very different from the small one. If you use symbols such as S and s or P and p, it can become difficult to tell them apart if they are written down quickly.

SAQ 5.4

In mice, the gene for eye colour has two alleles. The allele for black eyes is dominant, while the allele for red eyes is recessive.

Choose suitable symbols for these alleles, and then draw a genetic diagram to show the probable results of a cross between a heterozygous black-eyed mouse and a red-eyed mouse.

SAQ 5.5

A species of poppy may have plain petals, or petals with a large black spot near the base. If two plants with spotted petals are crossed, the offspring always have spotted petals. A cross between unspotted and spotted plants sometimes produces offspring which all have unspotted petals, and sometimes produces half spotted and half unspotted offspring. Explain these results.

Test crosses

Where alleles show dominance, it is not possible to tell the genotype of an organism showing the dominant characteristic just by looking at it. A purple-stemmed tomato plant might have the genotype AA, or it might have the genotype Aa. To find out its genotype, it could be crossed with a green-stemmed tomato plant.

If its genotype is AA

Parents' phenotypes	purple	green
Parents' genotypes	AA	aa
Gametes' genotypes	(A)	(a)
Offspring	all Aa	
	purple	

If its genotype is Aa

Parents' phenotypes	purple	green
Parents' genotypes	Aa	aa
Gametes' genotypes	(A) or (a)	(a)
Offspring	Aa or aa	
	purple	green

So, from the colours of the offspring, you can tell the genotype of the purple parent. If any green offspring are produced, then the purple parent must have the genotype Aa.

This cross is called a **test cross**. A test cross always involves crossing an organism showing the dominant phenotype with one which is homozygous recessive. (You may come across the term 'backcross' in some books, but test cross is the better term to use.)

SAQ 5.6

In dalmatian dogs, the colour of the spots is determined by a gene which has two alleles. The allele for black spots is dominant, and the allele for brown spots is recessive.

A breeder wanted to know the genotype of a black-spotted bitch. She crossed her with a brown-spotted dog, and a litter of three puppies was produced, all of which were black. The breeder concluded that her bitch was homozygous for the allele for black spots. Was she right? Explain your answer.

Multiple alleles

So far, we have considered just two alleles, or varieties, of any one gene. Most genes, however, have more than two alleles. An example of this situation, known as **multiple alleles**, is the gene for human blood groups.

The four blood groups A, B, AB and O are determined by a single gene. Three alleles of this gene exist, I^A, I^B, and I^o. Of these, I^A and I^B are codominant, while I^o is recessive to both I^A and I^B. As a diploid cell can carry only two alleles, the possible genotypes and phenotypes are as shown in *table 5.2*.

Genotype	Blood group
I^{A}I^A	A
I^{A}I^B	AB
I^{A}I^o	A
I^{B}I^B	B
I^{B}I^o	B
I^{o}I^o	O

● *Table 5.2*

SAQ 5.7

A man of blood group B and a woman of blood group A have three children. One is group A, one group B and one group O. What are the genotypes of these five people?

SAQ 5.8

Coat colour in rabbits is determined by a gene with four alleles. The allele for agouti (normal) coat is dominant to all of the other three alleles. The allele for albino coat is recessive to the other three alleles. The allele for chinchilla (grey) coat is dominant to the allele for himalayan (white with black ears, nose, feet and tail) *(Figure 5.3)*.

a   Write down the **ten** possible genotypes for coat colour, and their phenotypes.

b   Draw genetic diagrams to explain each of the following.

   (i)   An albino rabbit is crossed with a chinchilla rabbit, producing offspring which are all chinchilla. Two of these chinchilla offspring are then crossed, producing 4 chinchilla offspring and 2 albino.

   (ii)   An agouti rabbit is crossed with a himalayan rabbit, producing 3 agouti offspring and 3 himalayan.

   (iii)   Two agouti rabbits produce a litter of 5 young, three of whom are agouti and two chinchilla. The two chinchilla young are then crossed, producing 4 chinchilla offspring and 1 himalayan.

● *Figure 5.3*   Colour variations in rabbits, caused by multiple alleles of a single gene: **a** agouti,   **b** albino,   **c** chinchilla,   **d** himalayan.

Sex inheritance

In humans, sex is determined by one of the 23 pairs of chromosomes. These chromosomes are called the **sex chromosomes**. The other 22 pairs are called **autosomes**.

The sex chromosomes differ from the autosomes in that the two sex chromosomes in a cell are not always alike. They do not always have the same genes in the same position, and so they are not always homologous. This is because there are two types of sex chromosome, known as the X and Y chromosomes, because of their shapes. The Y chromosome is much shorter than the X, and carries fewer genes. A person with two X chromosomes is female, while a person with one X and one Y chromosome is male.

SAQ 5.9

Draw a genetic diagram to explain why there is always an equal chance that a child will be male or female. (You can do this in just the same way as the other genetic diagrams you have drawn, but using symbols to represent whole chromosomes, not genes.)

As a woman has two X chromosomes, all of the gametes she produces have one X chromosome. A man produces equal numbers of gametes containing an X chromosome and a Y chromosome.

Sex linkage

The X chromosome contains many different genes. (You can see some of these in *figure 2.5* in *Foundation Biology*.) One of them is a gene which codes for the production of a protein needed for blood clotting, called **factor VIII**. There are two alleles of this gene, the dominant one **F** producing normal factor VIII, and the recessive one **f** resulting in lack of it. People who are homozygous for the recessive allele suffer from the disease haemophilia, in which the blood fails to clot properly.

The fact that this gene is on the X chromosome, and not on an autosome, affects the way that it is inherited. Females, who have two X chromosomes, have two copies of the gene. Males, however, who have only one X chromosome, have only one copy of the gene. Therefore, the possible genotypes for men and women are different. They are shown in *figure 5.4*.

The factor VIII gene is said to be **sex-linked**. A sex-linked gene is one which is found on a part of the X chromosome not matched by the Y, and therefore not found on the Y chromosome.

Genotypes including sex-linked genes are always represented by symbols which show that they are on an X chromosome. Thus the genotype of a woman who has the allele F on one of her X chromosomes and the allele f on the other is written as $X^F X^f$.

You can draw genetic diagrams to show how sex-linked genes are inherited in exactly the same way as for other genes. For example, the following diagram shows the children that could be born to a couple where the man does not have haemophilia, while the woman is a carrier for the disease.

Parents' phenotypes	normal man	carrier woman
Parents' genotypes	$X^F Y$	$X^F X^f$
Gametes' genotypes	X^F or Y	X^F or X^f

Offspring genotypes and phenotypes

		Gametes from woman	
		X^F	X^f
Gametes from man	X^F	$X^F X^F$ normal female	$X^F X^f$ carrier female
	Y	$X^F Y$ normal male	$X^f Y$ haemophiliac male

Each time this couple have a child, therefore, there is a 0.25 probability that it will be a normal girl, a 0.25 probability that it will be a normal boy, a 0.25 probability that it will be a carrier girl and a 0.25 probability that it will be a boy with haemophilia.

SAQ 5.10

Can a man with haemophilia pass on the disease to:

a his son?

b his grandson?

Draw genetic diagrams to explain your answers.

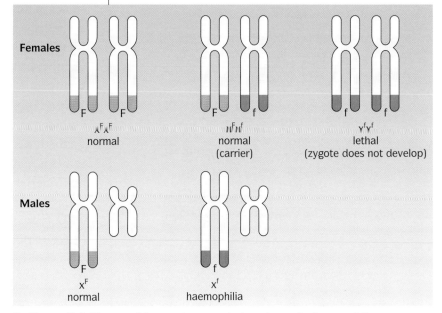

Females	$X^F X^F$ normal	$X^F X^f$ normal (carrier)	$X^f X^f$ lethal (zygote does not develop)		
Males	X^F normal	X^f haemophilia			

● **Figure 5.4** The possible genotypes and phenotypes for haemophilia.

SAQ 5.11

One of the genes for colour vision in humans is found on the X chromosome, but not on the Y chromosome. The dominant allele of this gene gives normal colour vision, while a recessive allele produces red–green colour blindness.

a Choose suitable symbols for these alleles, and then write down all of the possible genotypes for a man and for a woman.

b A couple who both have normal colour vision have a child with colour blindness. Explain how this may happen, and state what the sex of the colour blind child must be.

c Is it possible for a colour blind girl to be born? Explain your answer.

SAQ 5.12

One of the genes for coat colour in cats is sex-linked. The allele C^O gives orange fur, while C^B gives black fur. The two alleles are codominant, and when both are present the cat has patches of orange and black, which is known as tortoiseshell.

a Explain why male cats cannot be tortoiseshell.

b Draw a genetic diagram to show the expected genotypes and phenotypes of the offspring from a cross between an orange male and a tortoiseshell female cat. (Remember to show the X and Y chromosomes, as well as the symbols for the alleles.)

Dihybrid crosses

So far, we have considered the inheritance of just one gene. Such examples are called **monohybrid crosses**. **Dihybrid crosses** look at the inheritance of two genes at once.

You have already seen that, in tomato plants, there is a gene which codes for stem colour. This gene has two alleles:

stem colour gene

A = allele for purple stem
a = allele for green stem
where A is dominant and a is recessive.

A different gene, at a different locus on a different chromosome, codes for leaf shape. Again, there are two alleles:

leaf shape gene

D = allele for cut leaves
(jagged edges)
d = allele for potato leaves
(smooth edges)
where D is dominant and d is recessive.

What will happen if a plant which is heterozygous for both of these genes is crossed with a plant with green stem and potato leaves?

Figure 5.5 shows the alleles in a cell of the plant which is heterozygous for both genes. When this

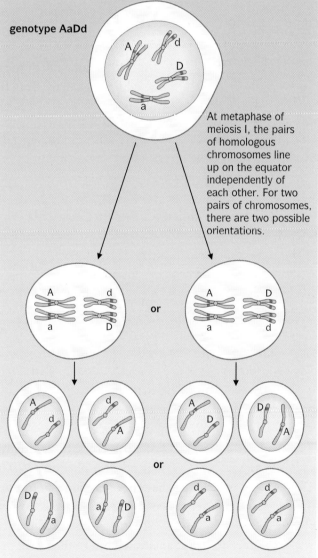

genotype AaDd

At metaphase of meiosis I, the pairs of homologous chromosomes line up on the equator independently of each other. For two pairs of chromosomes, there are two possible orientations.

or

or

At the end of meiosis II each orientation gives two types of gamete. There are therefore four types of gamete altogether.

● *Figure 5.5* Independent assortment of homologous chromosomes during meiosis I results in a variety of genotypes in the gametes formed.

cell undergoes meiosis to produce gametes, there are two possible ways in which the two pairs of chromosomes may line up on the equator during metaphase. If there are many such cells undergoing meiosis, then the chromosomes in roughly half of them will probably line up one way, and the other half will line up the other way. We can therefore predict that the gametes formed from these heterozygous cells will be of four types, **AD**, **Ad**, **aD** and **ad**, each occurring in approximately equal numbers.

The plant with green stem and potato leaves must have the genotype **aadd**. Each of its gametes will contain one **a** allele and one **d** allele. All of the gametes will have the genotype **ad**.

Parents' phenotypes	purple stem, cut leaves	green stem, potato leaves
Parents' genotypes	AaDd	aadd
Gametes' genotypes	AD or Ad or aD or ad	all ad
	in equal proportions	

At fertilisation, any of the four types of gamete from the heterozygous parent may fuse with the gametes from the homozygous parent. The genotypes of the offspring will be:

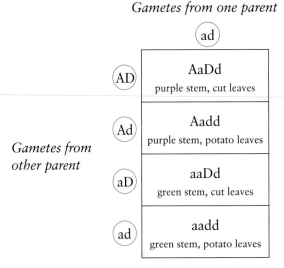

From this cross, therefore, we would expect approximately equal numbers of the four possible phenotypes. This **1:1:1:1** ratio is typical of a dihybrid cross between a heterozygous and a homozygous recessive organism, where the alleles show complete dominance.

If *both* parents are heterozygous, then things become a little more complicated, because both of them will produce four kinds of gametes.

Parents' phenotypes	purple stem, cut leaves	purple stem, cut leaves
Parents' genotypes	AaDd	AaDd
Gametes' genotypes	(AD) or (Ad) or (aD) or (ad)	(AD) or (Ad) or (aD) or (ad)
	in equal proportions	in equal proportions

Offspring genotypes and phenotypes

Gametes from one parent

	(AD)	(Ad)	(aD)	(ad)
(AD)	AADD purple, cut	AADd purple, cut	AaDD purple, cut	AaDd purple, cut
(Ad)	AADd purple, cut	AAdd purple, potato	AaDd purple, cut	Aadd purple, potato
(aD)	AaDD purple, cut	AaDd purple, cut	aaDD green, cut	aaDd green, cut
(ad)	AaDd purple, cut	Aadd purple, potato	aaDd green, cut	aadd green, potato

Gametes from other parent (left label)

If you sort out the numbers of each phenotype amongst these sixteen possibilities, you will find that the offspring would be expected to occur in the following ratio:

9 purple, cut : 3 purple, potato : 3 green, cut : 1 green, potato.

This **9:3:3:1** ratio is typical of a dihybrid cross between two heterozygous organisms, where the two alleles show complete dominance.

SAQ 5.13

Draw genetic diagrams to show the genotypes of the offspring from each of the following crosses.

a AABb × aabb

b GgHh × gghh

c TTyy × ttYY

d eeFf × Eeff

SAQ 5.14

The allele for grey fur in a species of animal is dominant to white, and the allele for long tail is dominant to short.

a Using the symbols G and g for coat colour, and T and t for tail length, draw a genetic diagram to show the genotypes and phenotypes of the offspring you would expect from a cross between a pure-breeding grey animal with a long tail and a pure-breeding white animal with a short tail.

b If this first generation of offspring were bred together, what would be the expected phenotypes in the second generation of offspring, and in what ratios would they occur?

In a species of plant, the allele for tall stem is dominant to short. The two alleles for leaf colour, giving green or white in the homozygous condition, are codominant, producing variegated leaves in the heterozygote.

A plant with tall stems and green leaves was crossed with a plant with short stems and variegated leaves. The offspring from this cross consisted of plants with tall stems and green leaves and plants with tall stems and variegated leaves in the ratio of 1 : 1. Construct a genetic diagram to explain this cross.

In a species of animal, it is known that the allele for black eyes is dominant to the allele for red eyes, and that the allele for long fur is dominant to the allele for short fur.

a What are the possible genotypes for an animal with black eyes and long fur?

b How could you find out which genotype this animal had?

Polygenes

So far in this chapter, we have considered characteristics which are determined by just one gene. Often, however, several genes at different loci determine a particular characteristic. An example is height in humans.

Several such genes, at different loci on different chromosomes, determine human height. Each of these genes has a number of alleles, so there is a large number of possible combinations of alleles. Each gene has a small effect on height. The overall effect of these genes depends on the additive effects of all the different alleles in a person's cells. As there are many different genes and many different alleles, there are many different possible combinations, so people come in many different heights (*figure 5.6*).

These genes are described as **polygenes**, and their inheritance as **polygenic inheritance**. Polygenes are a number of genes at different loci, which together produce an additive effect on a single characteristic in the phenotype of an organism.

Environment and phenotype

In all the examples in this chapter, we have so far assumed that the genotype of the organism will always affect its phenotype in the same way. This is not always true.

Consider human height. If you have inherited a number of alleles for tallness from your parents, you have the *potential* to grow tall. However, if your diet is poor while you are growing, your cells might not be supplied with sufficient nutrients to allow you to develop this potential. You will not grow as tall as you could. Part of your environment, your diet, has also affected your height. Many characteristics of organisms are affected by both genes and environment.

Another example is the development of the dark tips to ears, nose, paws and tail in the himalayan colouring of rabbits (*figure 5.3*). This colouring is caused by an allele which allows the formation of

● *Figure 5.6* Variation in human height is caused by both genotype and environment. Many different genes, each with different alleles, are involved. The result is continuous variation, with any height being possible between the upper and lower extremes.

the dark pigment only at low temperature. The parts of the rabbit which grow dark fur are the coldest parts. If an area somewhere else on its body is plucked of fur and kept cold, the new fur growing in this region will be dark.

A third example of the interaction between genes and environment concerns the bacterium *Escherichia coli*. This bacterium can be grown on nutrient agar jelly, where it secretes enzymes to digest the various nutrients in the jelly. The enzymes are synthesised by following the codes on the bacterium's genes.

E. coli has genes which code for the synthesis of the enzymes **lactose permease**, which enables the cell to take up lactose, and β **galactosidase**, which hydrolyses lactose to glucose and galactose. If the bacterium is grown on a medium containing only glucose, it does not produce either of these enzymes. If it is then transferred to a medium containing only lactose, the genes are 'switched on', and both lactose permease and β galactosidase are synthesised. The genes for these two enzymes have given the bacterium the *potential* to produce them, but it will only do so when the environmental conditions are right.

SAQ 5.17 _____

What advantage is it to *E. coli* to switch on its lactose permease and β galactosidase genes only when it is growing on a lactose-containing medium?

SUMMARY

- Diploid organisms contain two copies of each gene in each of their cells. In sexual reproduction, gametes are formed containing one copy of each gene. Each offspring receives two copies of each gene, one from each of its parents.

- Different varieties of a gene are called alleles. Alleles may show dominance or codominance. An organism possessing two identical alleles of a gene is homozygous; an organism possessing two different alleles of a gene is heterozygous. If a gene has several different alleles, such as the gene for human blood groups, these are known as multiple alleles.

- A gene found on the X chromosome but not on the Y chromosome is known as a sex-linked gene.

- The genotype of an organism showing dominant characteristics can be determined by looking at the offspring produced when it is crossed with an organism showing recessive characteristics. This is called a test cross.

- An organism which is heterozygous for two genes will produce gametes containing all four possible combinations of alleles in equal proportions. This independent assortment of alleles produces variation between offspring, and between offspring and their parents. Variation is also produced because any gamete from one parent may fuse with any gamete from the other.

- The genotype of an organism gives it the potential to show a particular characteristic. In many cases, the degree to which this characteristic is shown is also affected by the organism's environment.

Questions

1 For each of the following, discuss whether genotype or environment is more important in determining the phenotype of a human.
  a Height **b** Blood group **c** Shoe size
  d Athletic ability **e** How good you are at maths

2 Describe the ways in which sexual reproduction can bring about variation between individuals.

3 When mutation produces a new allele of a gene, it is usually recessive and harmful. Explain why:
  a it is advantageous for organisms to be diploid rather than haploid;
  b mutations do not usually appear in the phenotype of organisms until many generations after the mutation occurred;
  c inbreeding (breeding between close relatives) in humans is discouraged.

Chapter six

Evolution

By the end of this chapter you should be able to:

1 explain how variation is produced in sexually reproducing organisms;

2 understand that new variants of a gene may be
produced by mutation;

3 explain why variation caused by genes can be inherited, but variation caused by the environment cannot;

4 explain how most organisms have the reproductive
potential to increase their populations;

5 explain that, as no populations increase in size for
ever, many individuals must die before reaching their
full reproductive potential;

6 describe how different selection pressures may act on
individual organisms with different alleles, so that one
genotype is more likely to survive and reproduce than
another;

7 explain, with examples, how natural selection may
cause a change in allele frequencies;

8 explain the meaning of the term *species*, and describe
how natural selection may produce new species;

9 describe the classification of species into taxonomic
groups;

10 describe and explain one example of artificial
selection.

Variation

In chapter 5, you have seen how sexual reproduction produces genetic variation amongst the individuals in a population. Genetic variation is caused by:

■ independent assortment of chromosomes, and
therefore alleles, during meiosis;

■ crossing over between chromatids of homologous chromosomes during meiosis (this
process is explained in *Foundation Biology*);

■ random mating between organisms within a
species;

■ random fertilisation of gametes;

■ mutation.

The first four of these processes reshuffle alleles in
the population. Offspring have combinations of
alleles which differ from those of their parents,
and from each other. This genetic variation
produces phenotypic variation.

Mutation, however, does more than reshuffle
alleles which are already present. Mutation can
produce completely new alleles. This may happen,
for example, if a mistake occurs in DNA replication,
so that a new base sequence occurs in a gene. This is
probably how the sickle cell allele of the gene for
the production of the β polypeptide of haemoglobin
first arose. Such a change in a gene, which is quite
unpredictable, is called a **gene mutation**. The new
allele is very often recessive, so it frequently does
not show up in the population until some generations after the mutation actually occurred.

Mutations which occur in body, or **somatic**, cells
often have no effects at all on the organism. A
malfunctioning cell in a tissue is only one of thousands of similar cells, and it is very unlikely that
this cell would cause any problems. Most mutated
cells are recognised as foreign by the body's
immune systems and are destroyed. Occasionally
the mutation may affect the regulation of cell
division. If this cell escapes the attack of the
immune system, it can produce a lump of cells
called a tumour. Tumours often cause little harm,
but sometimes the tumour cells are able to spread
around the body and invade other tissues. This
type of tumour is described as **malignant**, and the
diseases caused by such tumours are **cancers**.

Mutations in somatic cells cannot be passed on
to offspring by sexual reproduction. However,
mutations in cells in the ovaries or testes of an
animal, or in the ovaries or anthers of a plant, may
be inherited by offspring. If a cell containing a
mutation divides to form gametes, then the
gametes may also contain the mutated gene. If such
a gamete is one of the two which fuse to form a
zygote, then the mutated gene will also be in the
zygote. This single cell then divides repeatedly to

68

form a new organism, in which all the cells will contain the mutated gene.

Genetic variation, whether caused by the reshuffling of alleles during meiosis and sexual reproduction, or by the introduction of new alleles by mutation, can be passed on by parents to their offspring. Variation in phenotype is also caused by the *environment* in which organisms live. For example, some organisms might be larger than others, because they had access to better quality food while they were growing. This type of variation is not passed on by parents to their offspring.

SAQ 6.1

Explain why variation caused by the environment cannot be passed from an organism to its offspring.

Overproduction

All organisms have the reproductive potential to increase their populations. Rabbits, for example, produce several young in a litter, and each female may produce several litters each year. If all the young rabbits survived to adulthood and reproduced, then the rabbit population would rapidly increase. *Figure 6.1* shows what might happen.

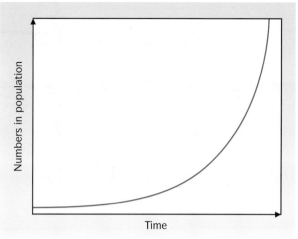

● *Figure 6.1* If unchecked by environmental factors, numbers in a population may increase exponentially.

This sort of population growth actually did happen in Australia in the nineteenth century. In 1859, twelve pairs of rabbits from Britain were released on a ranch in Victoria, as a source of food. The rabbits found conditions to their liking. Rabbits feed on low growing vegetation, especially grasses, of which there was an abundance. There were very few predators to feed on them, so the number of rabbits soared. Their numbers became so great that they seriously affected the availability of grazing for sheep *(figure 6.2)*.

● *Figure 6.2* Attempts to control the rabbit population explosion in Australia in the mid to late nineteenth century included 'rabbit drives', in which huge numbers were rounded up and killed. Eventually, myxomatosis brought numbers down.

Such population explosions are rare in normal circumstances. Although rabbit populations have the potential to increase at such a tremendous rate, they do not usually do so.

As a population of rabbits increases, various **environmental factors** come into play to keep down their numbers. These factors may be **biotic**, that is caused by other living organisms such as predation, competition for food, or infection by pathogens; or they may be **abiotic**, that is caused by non-living components of the environment such as water supply or nutrient levels in the soil. For example, the increasing number of rabbits eats an increasing amount of vegetation, until food is in short supply. The larger population may allow the populations of predators, such as foxes, stoats and weasels, to increase. Overcrowding may occur, increasing the ease with which diseases such as myxomatosis *(figure 6.3)* may spread. This disease is caused by a virus which is transmitted by fleas. The closer together the rabbits live, the more easily fleas, and therefore viruses, will pass from one rabbit to another.

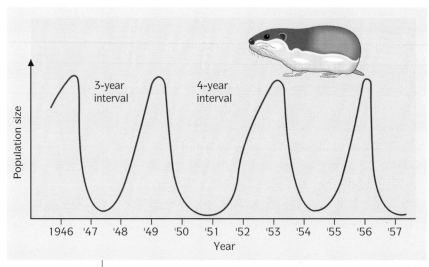

● *Figure 6.4* Lemming populations are famous for their large increases and decreases. In some years, populations become so large that lemmings may emigrate 'en masse' from overcrowded areas. The reason for the oscillating population size is not known for certain, although it has been suggested that food supply or food quality may be the main cause. As the population size rises, food supplies run out, so the population size crashes. Once the population size has decreased, food supplies begin to recover, and the population size rises again.

These environmental factors act to reduce the rate of growth of the rabbit population. Of all the rabbits born, many will die from lack of food, or be killed by predators, or die from myxomatosis. Only a small proportion of young will grow to adulthood and reproduce, so population growth slows.

If the pressure of the environmental factors is sufficiently great, then the population size will decrease. Only when the numbers of rabbits have fallen considerably will the numbers be able to grow again. Over a period of time, the population will oscillate about a mean level. *Figure 6.4* shows this kind of pattern in a lemming population over eleven years. The oscillations in lemming populations are particularly marked; in other populations, they are usually less spectacular!

This type of pattern is shown by the populations of many organisms. The number of young produced is far greater than the number which will survive to adulthood. Many young die before reaching reproductive age.

● *Figure 6.3* Rabbits living in dense populations are more likely to get myxomatosis than those in less crowded conditions.

Natural selection

What determines which will be the few rabbits to survive, and which will die? It may be just luck. However, some rabbits will be born with a better chance of survival than others. Variation within a population of rabbits means that some will have features which give them an advantage in the 'struggle for existence'.

One feature which may vary is coat colour. Most rabbits have alleles which give the normal agouti colour. A few, however, may be homozygous for the recessive allele which gives white coat. Such white rabbits will stand out distinctly from the others, and are more likely to be picked out by a predator such as a fox. They are less likely to survive than agouti rabbits. The chances of a white rabbit reproducing and passing on its white alleles to its offspring are very small, so the white allele will remain very rare in the population.

Predation by foxes is an example of a **selection pressure**. Selection pressures increase the chances of some alleles being passed on to the next generation, and decrease the chances of others. In this case, the agouti alleles have a selective advantage over the white alleles. The agouti alleles will remain the commoner alleles in the population, while the white alleles will remain very rare. The white alleles may even disappear completely.

The effects of such selection pressures on the frequency of alleles in a population is called **natural selection**. Natural selection raises the frequency of alleles conferring an advantage, and reduces the frequency of alleles conferring a disadvantage.

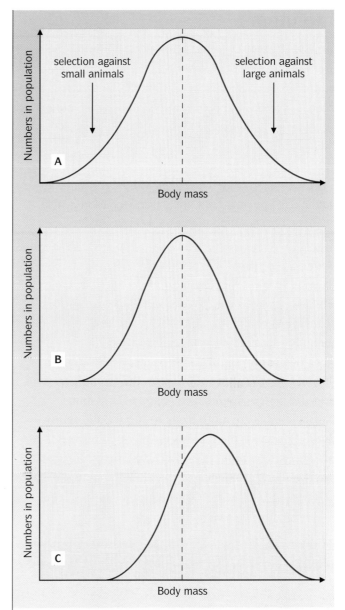

● *Figure 6.5* If a characteristic in a population, such as body mass, shows wide variation, selection pressures often act against the two extremes (graph **A**). Very small or very large individuals are less likely to survive and reproduce than those whose size lies nearer the centre of the range. This results in a population with a narrower range of body size (graph **B**). This type of selection, which tends to keep the variation in a characteristic centred around the same mean value, is called **stabilising selection**.

Graph **C** shows what would happen if selection acted against smaller individuals but not larger ones. In this case, the range of variation shifts towards larger size. This type of selection, which results in a change in a characteristic in a particular direction, is called **directional selection**.

SAQ 6.2

Skomer is a small island off the coast of Wales. Rabbits have been living on the island for many years. There are no predators on the island.

a Rabbits on Skomer are not all agouti. There are quite large numbers of rabbits of different colours, such as black and white. Suggest why this is so.

b What do you think might be important selection pressures acting on rabbits on Skomer?

Evolution

Usually, natural selection keeps things the way they are. This is **stabilising selection**. Agouti rabbits are best adapted to survive predation, so the agouti allele remains the most common coat colour allele in rabbit populations. Unless something changes, then natural selection will ensure that this continues to be the case.

However, if a *new environmental factor*, or a *new allele* appears, then allele frequencies may also change. This is called **directional selection**.

A new environmental factor

Imagine that we were plunged into a new Ice Age. The climate becomes much colder, so that snow covers the ground for almost all of the year. Assuming that rabbits can cope with these conditions, white rabbits now have a selective advantage during seasons when snow lies on the ground, as they are better camouflaged (*figure 6.7*). Rabbits with white fur are more likely to survive and reproduce, passing on their alleles for white fur to their offspring. The frequency of the allele for white coat increases, at the expense of the allele for agouti. Over many generations, almost all rabbits will come to have white coats rather than agouti.

● *Figure 6.6* The tuatara, *Sphenodon punctatus*, is a lizard-like reptile which lives in New Zealand. Fossils of a virtually identical animal have been found in rocks 200 million years old. Natural selection has acted to keep the features of this organism the same over all this time.

● *Figure 6.7* The white winter coat of a mountain hare provides excellent camouflage from predators, against snow.

A new allele

Most mutations which occur, because they are random events, produce features which are harmful. That is, they produce organisms which are less well adapted to their environment than 'normal' organisms. Other mutations may be 'neutral', conferring neither an advantage nor a disadvantage on the organisms within which they occur. Occasionally mutations may produce useful features.

Imagine that a mutation occurs in the coat colour gene of a rabbit, producing a new allele which gives a better camouflaged coat colour than agouti. Rabbits possessing this new allele will have a selective advantage. They will be more likely to survive and reproduce than agouti rabbits, so the new allele will become more common in the population. Over many generations, almost all rabbits will come to have the new allele.

Such changes in allele frequency in a population are the basis of **evolution**. Evolution occurs as natural selection gives some alleles a better chance of survival than others. Over many generations, populations may gradually change, becoming better adapted to their environments. Examples of such change are the development of antibiotic resistance in bacteria and industrial melanism in *Biston betularia*.

Antibiotic resistance

Antibiotics are chemicals which inhibit or kill bacteria, but do not normally harm human tissue. Most antibiotics are produced by fungi. The first antibiotic to be discovered was penicillin, which was first used during the Second World War to treat a wide range of diseases caused by bacteria. Penicillin stops cell wall formation in bacteria, so preventing cell reproduction.

If someone takes penicillin to treat a bacterial infection, bacteria which are sensitive to penicillin will die. In most cases, this will be the entire population of the disease-causing bacteria. However, by chance, there may be among them one or more individual bacteria with an allele giving resistance to penicillin. One example of such an allele occurs in some populations of the bacterium *Staphylococcus*, where some individuals produce an enzyme, penicillinase, which inactivates penicillin.

As bacteria have only one chromosome, they have only one copy of each gene, so the mutant allele will have an immediate effect on the phenotype of any bacterium possessing it. These individuals have a tremendous selective advantage. The bacteria without this allele will be killed, while those bacteria with resistance can survive and reproduce. Bacteria reproduce very rapidly in ideal conditions, and even if there was initially only one resistant bacterium, it might produce ten thousand million descendants within 24 hours. A large population of a penicillin-resistant strain of *Staphylococcus* would result.

Such antibiotic-resistant strains of bacteria are continually appearing. By using antibiotics, we change the environmental factors which exert selection pressures on bacteria. A constant 'arms race' is on to find new antibiotics against new resistant strains of bacteria.

Alleles for antibiotic resistance often occur on plasmids (see page 52). Plasmids are quite frequently transferred from one bacterium to another, even between different species. Thus it is even possible for resistance to a particular antibiotic to arise in one species of bacterium, and be passed on to another. The more we use antibiotics, the greater the selection pressure we exert on bacteria to evolve resistance to them.

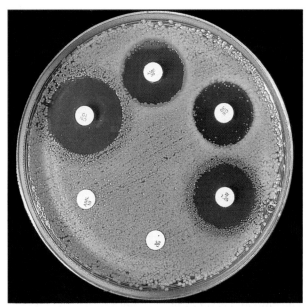

● *Figure 6.8* The grey areas on the agar jelly in this petri dish are colonies of the bacterium *Escherichia coli*. The white discs are pieces of card impregnated with different antibiotics. Where there are clear areas around the disc, the antibiotic has prevented the bacteria from growing. However, you can see that this strain of *E. coli* is resistant to the antibiotics on the discs at the bottom left and has been able to grow right up to the discs.

SAQ 6.3

Suggest how each of the following might decrease the chances of an antibiotic-resistant strain of bacteria developing:

a limiting the use of antibiotics to cases where there is a real need;

b regularly changing the type of antibiotic which is prescribed for a particular disease;

c using two or more antibiotics together to treat a bacterial infection.

Industrial melanism

One well-documented case of the way in which changing environmental factors may produce changes in allele frequencies is in the peppered moth, *Biston betularia (figure 6.9)*. This is a night-flying moth, which spends the day resting on tree trunks. It relies on camouflage to protect it from insect-eating birds which hunt by sight. Until 1849, all specimens of this moth in collections had pale

● **Figure 6.9** Light and melanic forms of peppered moths on light and dark tree bark.

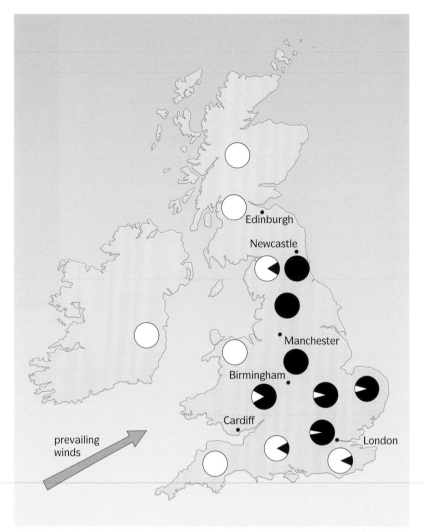

prevailing winds

● **Figure 6.10** The distribution of the pale and dark forms of the peppered moth, *Biston betularia*, in the early 1960s. The ratio of dark to light areas in each circle shows the ratio of dark to light moths in that part of the country.

wings with dark markings, giving a speckled appearance. In 1849, however, a black (melanic) individual was caught near Manchester. During the rest of the nineteenth century, the numbers of black *Biston betularia* increased dramatically in some areas, while in other parts of the country the speckled form remained the more common.

The difference in the black and speckled forms of the moth is caused by a single gene. The normal speckled colouring is produced by a recessive allele of this gene, c, while the black colour is produced by a dominant allele, C. The frequency of the allele C has increased in areas near to industrial cities. In non-industrial areas, the allele c has remained the more common allele *(figure 6.10)*.

The selection pressure causing the change of allele frequency in industrial areas is predation by birds. In areas with unpolluted air, tree trunks are often covered with grey, brown and green lichen. On such tree trunks, speckled moths are superbly camouflaged.

However, lichens are very sensitive to pollutants such as sulphur dioxide, and do not grow on trees near to or downwind of industries releasing pollutants into the air. Trees in these areas therefore have much darker bark, against which the dark moths are better camouflaged. Experiments have shown that light moths have a much higher chance of survival in unpolluted areas than dark moths, while in polluted areas the dark moths have the selective advantage. As air pollution from industry is reduced, the selective advantage swings back in favour of the speckled variety. So we would expect the proportion of speckled moths to increase if we succeeded in reducing the output of certain pollutants. This is, in fact, what has happened since the 1970s.

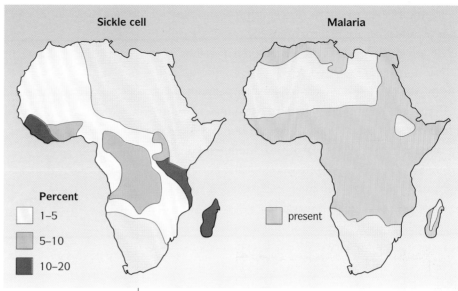

It is important to realise that the C allele has probably been present in *B. betularia* populations for a very long time. It has not been produced by pollution. Until the nineteenth century there was such a strong selection pressure against the C allele that it remained exceedingly rare. Mutations of the c allele to the C allele may have occurred quite frequently, but moths with this allele would almost certainly have been eaten by birds before they could reproduce. Changes in environmental factors only affect the likelihood of an allele surviving in a population; they do not affect the likelihood of such an allele arising by mutation.

Sickle cell anaemia

In chapter 4, you saw how an allele, H^S, of the gene which codes for the production of the β polypeptides of the haemoglobin molecule can produce sickling of red blood cells. People who are homozygous for this allele have sickle cell anaemia. This is a severe form of anaemia which is often lethal.

The possession of two copies of this allele obviously puts a person at a great selective disadvantage. People who are homozygous for the sickle cell allele are less likely to survive and reproduce. Until recently, almost everyone with sickle cell anaemia died before reaching reproductive age. Yet the frequency of the sickle cell allele is very high in some parts of the world. In some parts of East Africa, almost 50% of babies born are carriers for

● *Figure 6.11* The distribution of people with at least one copy of the sickle cell allele, and the distribution of malaria, in Africa.

this allele, and 14% are homozygous, suffering from sickle cell anaemia. How can this be explained?

The parts of the world where the sickle cell allele is most common are also the parts of the world where malaria is found *(figure 6.11)*. Malaria is caused by a protoctist parasite, *Plasmodium*, which can be introduced into a person's blood when an infected mosquito bites *(figure 6.12)*. The parasites enter red blood cells and multiply inside them. Malaria is the major source of illness and death in many parts of the world.

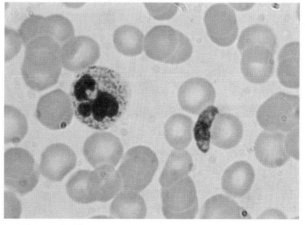

● *Figure 6.12* The crescent-shaped purple structure in this micrograph of human blood is a *Plasmodium*, the protoctist which causes malaria (× 1400). At an earlier stage in the life cycle of *Plasmodium*, the organism reproduces inside the red blood cells.

In studies carried out in Africa, it has been found that people who are heterozygous for the sickle cell allele are much less likely to suffer from a serious attack of malaria than people who are homozygous for the normal allele. Heterozygous people with malaria only have about one third the number of *Plasmodium* in their blood as normal homozygotes. In one study, of a sample of 100 children who died from malaria, all except one were normal homozygotes, although within the population as a whole 20% of people were heterozygotes.

There are, therefore, two strong selection pressures acting on these two alleles. Selection against people who are homozygous for the sickle cell allele, H^SH^S, is very strong, because they become seriously anaemic. Selection against people who are homozygous for the normal allele, H^NH^N, is also very strong, as they are more likely to die from malaria. In areas where malaria is common, heterozygotes, H^NH^S, have a strong selective advantage; they do not suffer from sickle cell anaemia and are much less likely to suffer badly from malaria. So both alleles remain in populations where malaria is an important environmental factor. In places where malaria was never present, selection against people with the genotype H^SH^S has almost completely removed the H^S allele from populations.

Artificial selection

Sometimes, the most important selection pressures on organisms are those applied by humans. When humans purposefully apply selection pressures to populations, the process is known as **artificial selection.**

Consider, for example, the development of modern breeds of cattle. Cattle have been domesticated for a very long time *(figure 6.13)*. For thousands of years, people have tried to 'improve' their cattle. Desired features include docility (making the animal easier to control), fast growth rates and high milk yields. Increases in these characteristics have been achieved by **selective breeding.** Individuals showing one or more of these features to a larger degree than other individuals have been chosen for breeding. Some of the alleles conferring

● ***Figure 6.13*** The original wild cattle from which individuals were first domesticated are thought to have looked very much like the modern Chillingham White breed (top). Selective breeding over many centuries has produced many different breeds, such as the Guernsey (below). Guernseys have been bred for the production of large quantities of fat-rich milk. Notice the large body size and large udder compared with the Chillingham.

these features are passed on to their offspring. Again, the 'best' animals from this generation are chosen for breeding. Over many generations, alleles conferring the desired characteristics will increase in frequency, while those conferring characteristics not desired by the breeder will decrease in frequency. In many cases, such 'disadvantageous' alleles are lost entirely.

The Darwin–Wallace theory of evolution by natural selection

The original theory that natural selection might be a mechanism by which evolution can occur was put forward independently by Charles Darwin and Alfred Russell Wallace in 1856. They knew nothing of genes or mutations, so did not understand how natural variation could arise or be inherited. Nevertheless, they realised the significance of variation. Their observations and deductions can be summarised briefly as follows:

Observation 1 Organisms produce more offspring than are needed to replace the parents.

Observation 2 Natural populations tend to remain stable in size over long periods.

Deduction 1 There is competition for survival (a 'struggle for existence').

Observation 3 There is variation among the individuals of a given species.

Deduction 2 The best adapted variants will be selected for by the natural conditions operating at the time. In other words, natural selection will occur. The 'best' variants have a selective advantage; 'survival of the fittest' occurs.

As you can see, this theory, put forward well over a century ago, hardly differs from what we now know about natural selection and evolution. The major difference is that we can now think of natural selection as selecting particular *alleles* or groups of alleles.

The title of Darwin's most famous and important book contained the words *On the Origin of Species*. Yet, despite his thorough consideration of how natural selection could cause evolution, he did not attempt to explain how *new species* could be produced. This process is called **speciation**.

Species and speciation

In this chapter, you have seen how natural selection can act on variation within a population to bring about changes in allele frequencies. Biologists believe that natural selection is the force which has produced all of the different species of organisms on Earth. Yet in the examples described on pages 73–5, that is the evolution of antibiotic resistance in bacteria, and changes in frequencies of wing colour in peppered moths, no new species have been produced. How can natural selection produce new species?

Before we can begin to answer this question, we must answer another: exactly what *is* a species? This proves to be an extremely difficult question, with no neat answer.

The definition of a species which is most widely accepted by biologists is *a group of organisms, with similar morphological, physiological and behavioural features, which can interbreed to produce fertile offspring, and are reproductively isolated from other species.* 'Morphological' features are structural features, while 'physiological' features are the way that the body works. Thus all donkeys look and work like donkeys, and can breed with other donkeys to produce more donkeys which themselves can interbreed. All donkeys belong to the same species. Donkeys can interbreed with organisms of another similar species, horses, to produce offspring called mules. However, mules are infertile; that is they cannot breed and are effectively a 'dead-end'. Thus donkeys and horses belong to different species.

When a decision needs to be made as to whether two organisms belong to the same species or to two different species, they should ideally be tested to find out if they can interbreed successfully, producing fertile offspring. However, as you can imagine, this is not always possible. Perhaps the organisms are dead; they may even be museum specimens or fossils. Perhaps they are both of the same sex. Perhaps the biologist making the decision does not have the time or the facilities to attempt to interbreed them. Perhaps the organisms will not breed in captivity. Perhaps they are not organisms which reproduce sexually, but only asexually. Perhaps they are immature, and not yet able to breed.

As a result of all of these problems, it is quite rare to test the ability of two organisms to interbreed. Biologists frequently rely only on morphological, physiological and behavioural differences to decide whether they are looking at specimens from one or two species. In practice, it may only be morphological features which are considered, because physiological, and to some extent behavioural, ones are more time-consuming to investigate.

It can be extremely difficult to decide when these features are sufficiently similar or different to decide whether two organisms should belong to the same or a different species. This leads to great uncertainties and disagreements about whether to lump many slightly different variations of organisms together into one species, or whether to split them up into many different species.

Speciation

Despite the problems described above, most biologists would agree that the feature which really decides whether or not two organisms belong to different species is their inability to interbreed successfully. In explaining how natural selection can produce new species, therefore, we must consider how a group of interbreeding organisms, and so all of the same species, can produce another group of organisms which cannot interbreed successfully with the first group. The two groups must become **reproductively isolated**.

Once again, this is not a question with a neat and straightforward answer. The main difficulty is that this process *takes time*. You cannot, at least not easily, set up a speciation experiment in a laboratory because it would have to run for many years. The evidence which we have for the ways in which speciation can occur is almost all circumstantial evidence. We can look at populations of organisms at one moment in time, that is now, and use the patterns we can see to suggest what might have happened, and might still be happening, over long periods of time.

One picture which emerges from this kind of observation is that **geographical isolation** has played a major role in the evolution of many species. This is suggested by the fact that many islands have their own unique groups of species. The Hawaiian and Galapagos islands, for example, are famous for their spectacular array of species of all kinds of animals and plants found nowhere else in the world.

Geographical isolation requires a barrier of some kind to arise between two populations of the same species, preventing them from mixing. This barrier might be a stretch of water. We can imagine that a group of organisms, perhaps a population of a species of bird, somehow arrived on one of the Hawaiian islands from mainland America; they might have been blown off course by a storm. Here, separated by hundreds of miles of ocean from the rest of their species on mainland America, the group interbred. The selection pressures on the island were very different from those on the mainland, resulting in different alleles being selected for. Over time, the morphological, physiological and behavioural features of the island population became so different from the mainland population that they could no longer interbreed. A new species had evolved.

You can probably think of many other ways in which two populations of a species could be physically separated. A species living in dense forest, for example, could become split if large areas of forest are cut down, leaving 'islands' of forest in a 'sea' of agricultural land. Very small or immobile organisms can be isolated by smaller scale barriers.

Classification

Biologists not only classify organisms into species, but also classify species into larger groups. The study of the classification of organisms is called **taxonomy**.

Organisms can be classified according to their evolutionary relationships. In order to do this, taxonomists look for shared **homologous features** between different organisms. These are features which appear to have similar underlying designs, and so have almost certainly evolved from the same 'original' design which existed in a particular organism at one stage. A classic example of homologous structures is the limb bones of vertebrates. In all birds and mammals, for example, these limb bones take the same general pattern, with a single bone in the upper limb and two bones in the lower limb (figure 6.14). You can always pick out this pattern, despite great variations in the way the pattern has been modified in the course of evolution. Such features supply strong evidence that all organisms possessing them had a common ancestor.

You have already seen the criteria which are used (or not used!) to classify organisms into a particular **species**. Species which share many homologous features, suggesting that they may have evolved from a common ancestor, are grouped into the same **genus**. Thus horses, donkeys and zebras all belong to the genus *Equus*. They have probably all evolved from what was a single species a long time ago.

Every species is given a two-word Latin name, called a **binomial**. This system was invented by Carl Linnaeus, a Swedish naturalist, in the early eighteenth century, when Latin was a language widely used by educated people all over Europe. Although some people find Latin names awkward, they are extremely useful to biologists, because their

use is very precise and universal. Thus a biologist in Malaysia and another in Britain both know exactly what organism they are talking about when they use the name *Equus burchelli*. (It is a particular species of zebra.)

The binomial is made up of the name of the organism's genus, followed by that of its species. The generic name is always given a capital letter, while that of the species has a small letter. Both are written in italics. When you are writing by hand,

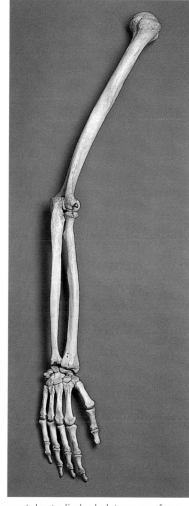

● *Figure 6.14* These three vertebrate limb skeletons are from a bird, a sheep and a human. They are homologous structures; each has the same basic design of a single bone in the upper part of the limb, and two bones in the lower part. This indicates that these three very different species shared a common ancestor, and so are related. Try to identify the different bones in each limb, and consider how the different relative shapes and sizes of these bones in each animal may adapt them to their way of life.

and cannot use italics, you should underline the binomial. To be really scientifically correct, a binomial should also include the name of the person who first named the organism, written in brackets. However, there is no need for you to do this, as it is of no use to anyone other than a professional taxonomist!

Genera (the plural of genus) are in turn grouped into **families**. Families are grouped into **orders**, orders into **classes**, classes into **phyla** (singular phylum) and phyla into **kingdoms**. Thus, a full classification of the common zebra is:

Kingdom	Animalia (non-photosynthetic, multicellular organisms)
Phylum	Chordata (animals with a stiffening rod along the back)
Class	Mammalia (chordates with hair and mammary glands)
Order	Perissodactyla (mammals with hooves made up of an odd number of toes)
Family	Equidae (horse-like perissodactyls)
Genus	*Equus* (horses, zebras and asses)
Species	*burchelli* (common zebra)

SUMMARY

■ Meiosis, random mating and the random fusion of gametes produce variation amongst populations of sexually reproducing organisms. Variation is also caused by the interaction of the environment with genetic factors, but such environmentally induced variation is not passed on to an organism's offspring. The only source of *new* alleles is mutation.

■ All species of organisms have the reproductive potential to increase the sizes of their populations, but, in the long term, this rarely happens. This is because environmental factors come into play to limit population growth. Such factors decrease the rate of reproduction, or increase the rate of mortality so that many individuals die before reaching reproductive age.

■ Within a population, certain alleles may increase the chance that an individual will survive long enough to be able to reproduce successfully. These alleles are therefore more likely to be passed on to the next generation than others. This is known as natural selection. Normally, natural selection keeps allele frequencies as they are; this is stabilising selection. However, if environmental factors which exert selection pressures change, or if new alleles appear in a population, then natural selection may cause a change in the frequencies of alleles; this is directional selection.

■ Over many generations, directional selection may produce large changes in allele frequencies. This is how evolution occurs.

■ If a population becomes isolated from the rest of its species, then the different selection pressures acting on it may, over time, result in such great morphological, physiological or behavioural changes between the two groups that they become incapable of interbreeding. This is one way in which new species can be formed.

■ Artificial selection occurs in the same way as natural selection, but here the selection pressures are exerted by humans on organisms which they wish to develop for their own use.

■ Organisms are classified according to their probable evolutionary relationships. Each species of organism is given a binomial, which is the name of its genus and species. Genera are further grouped into larger categories, in a hierarchy following the sequence genus, family, class, order, phylum and kingdom.

Questions

1 'Artificial selection of crop plants and farm animals has tended to reduce variety within their populations'. Discuss the validity of this statement, with reference to specific examples (you will need to research these), and consider the possible disadvantages of such a reduction in variation.

2 It is frequently found that individuals within populations of small mammals, such as mice or voles, which live on islands are larger than those living on the mainland; while those of large mammals, such as elephants and bears, tend to be smaller than those on the mainland. Suggest reasons for this.

Area		Dark form	Light form
unpolluted	released	473	496
	recaptured	30	62
polluted	released	601	201
	recaptured	205	32

3 The table shows the results of an experiment carried out to investigate the selection pressures acting on the dark and light forms of the moth *Biston betularia*. Dark and light moths were marked, and then released in two different areas. They were then recaptured by attracting them to a light at night.

a What percentage of dark moths were recaptured in (i) the unpolluted area and (ii) the polluted area?

b What percentage of light moths were recaptured in (i) the unpolluted area and (ii) the polluted area?

c The selection pressure on these two forms of the moth is thought to be predation by birds. Suggest a way in which you could investigate whether this is true.

d From these results, in which of the two areas does the selection pressure appear to be greater? Suggest what this might mean in terms of the rate of change of allele frequencies in polluted and unpolluted areas.

Appendix

The table shows the triplets of bases in a DNA molecule which code for each amino acid.

First position	Second position				Third position
	A	**G**	**T**	**C**	
A	Phe	Ser	Tyr	Cys	A
	Phe	Ser	Tyr	Cys	G
	Leu	Ser	STOP	STOP	T
	Leu	Ser	STOP	Trp	C
G	Leu	Pro	His	Arg	A
	Leu	Pro	His	Arg	G
	Leu	Pro	Gln	Arg	T
	Leu	Pro	Gln	Arg	C
T	Ile	Thr	Asn	Ser	A
	Ile	Thr	Asn	Ser	G
	Ile	Thr	Lys	Arg	T
	Met	Thr	Lys	Arg	C
C	Val	Ala	Asp	Gly	A
	Val	Ala	Asp	Gly	G
	Val	Ala	Glu	Gly	T
	Val	Ala	Glu	Gly	C

Answers to self-assessment questions

Chapter 1

1.1 **a** Both chlorophyll *a* and *b* have absorption peaks in the blue (450–5 nm) and red (650–700 nm) wavelengths. The carotenoids also have a peak at about 450 nm.

The action spectrum also peaks in the blue and red wavelengths. It is these absorbed wavelengths that provide energy for photosynthesis.

b Different pigments have different absorption spectra.

The maxima of the action spectrum most closely match the absorption spectrum of chlorophyll *a*. Although the peaks at the two ends of the spectrum are of similar height, the action spectrum has a larger peak at 700 nm. These wavelengths have more energy.

The peaks of the action spectrum are broader than those of the chlorophyll *a* absorption spectrum because of the light absorbed by other pigments.

The action spectrum does not perfectly match the absorption spectra since not all absorbed light is used in photosynthesis.

1.2 **a** The chloroplasts absorb light and split water (photolysis) generating hydrogen ions. This reduces DCPIP from blue to colourless, so that the colorimeter reading falls.

b The chloroplasts in light reduce DCPIP at a steady rate. The chloroplasts in the dark for five minutes do not reduce DCPIP during that time. When placed in the light, reduction occurs at a slightly slower rate. (A possible reason for this is gradual loss of activity by isolated chloroplasts because of damage.)

1.3 The Hill reaction shows that chloroplasts have 'reducing power' necessary to reduce fixed carbon dioxide to carbohydrate. They produce hydrogen ions. This is seen by their reduction of a coloured redox agent (blue DCPIP) to colourless.

1.4 **a** Experiments 1 and 2 differ only in temperature and show the limiting effect of temperature. Rate is approximately doubled by 10 °C temperature rise, both in initial increase in light intensity and at light saturation. Effect is via the light-independent stage since increased temperature increases the rate of these reactions.

b Experiments 1 and 3 differ in carbon dioxide concentration and show limiting effect of that concentration. A tenfold increase of external carbon dioxide concentration produces an approximate doubling of rate. Limiting effect is not only external carbon dioxide concentration but the rate at which the leaf can be supplied with carbon dioxide. This depends on the steepness of the diffusion gradient and the permeability of the leaf.

Chapter 2

2.1 The sequence of reactions generates an acceptor molecule which allows the sequence to occur again.

By decarboxylation, citrate, a six-carbon compound, can be converted to five-carbon and four-carbon compounds, finally giving oxaloacetate which can act as an acceptor for an incoming two-carbon unit from acetylcoenzyme A giving citrate again.

2.2 Reduced NAD per glucose:

from glycolysis	2
from the link reaction (1 × 2)	2
from the Krebs cycle (3 × 2)	6
Total	10

Reduced FAD per glucose:

from the Krebs cycle (1 × 2)	2

Remember that two molecules of pyruvate go through the link reaction, and that there are two turns of the Krebs cycle, for each molecule of glucose respired.

2.3 Each reduced NAD produces 3ATP in oxidative phosphorylation; each reduced FAD produces 2ATP.

Oxidative phosphorylation gives 34ATP per molecule of glucose, as follows:

via 2 reduced NAD from glycolysis (2 × 3)	6
via 2 reduced NAD from the link reaction (2 × 3)	6
via 2 reduced FAD from the Krebs cycle (2 × 2)	4
via 6 reduced NAD from the Krebs cycle (6 × 3)	18

2.4 Only 2ATP (1ATP per turn) are made directly in the Krebs cycle.

Hydrogen atoms are lost at four different stages of each turn of the cycle. Once these have been taken up by hydrogen carriers, they can be transferred to the reactions of oxidative phosphorylation to give much more ATP.

2.5 Points should include: the link reaction and Krebs cycle take place in the liquid matrix where enzymes and substrates can freely interact; mitochondria in active tissues are large and have many cristae; the large surface area of cristae for the layout of the sequences/'production lines' of carriers needed for electron transfer; the importance of the membranes and the intermembrane space for building up a hydrogen ion gradient in chemiosmosis; the role of ATP synthetase.

Chapter 3

3.1 These animals are homeothermic, generating heat within their cells to keep their body temperature constant. This body temperature is normally above the environmental temperature, and so large quantities of heat are lost from their bodies.

3.2 **a** $38\,000\,kJ\,m^{-2}\,year^{-1}$, $31\,000\,kJ\,m^{-2}\,year^{-1}$

b $54\,000\,kJ\,m^{-2}\,year^{-1}$

c For example, higher light intensity, higher temperatures and higher rainfall allow photosynthesis to take place at a greater rate; there are few seasonal variations in these factors, so photosynthesis can continue all the year round; coniferous trees in the pine forest must be adapted to withstand cold and water shortage in winter, so have narrow needles, limiting maximum rates of light absorption even when environmental conditions are ideal for photosynthesis; tropical rain forest has a greater density of plants.

d Alfalfa plants are young and growing, so much of the carbon they fix in photosynthesis is incorporated into new cells rather than being respired. In the rain forest, the trees are mostly mature and amounts of growth will be small. Alfalfa is a nitrogen-fixer and this, together with the probable application of fertiliser to the crop, could allow greater rates of growth than in the rain forest or pine forest.

3.3 The areas of the boxes in the pyramid should be drawn accurately in the proportion 14:42:124, with tertiary consumers at the top.

3.4 **a** $117\,kJ\,m^{-2}$

b The overall shape of each pyramid is very similar. However, the ratio of energy in one moment of time in producers and primary consumers is about 22, while the same ratio for energy flow is about 35. This means that the relative rate of energy flow is a little greater for producers than for primary consumers. The producers (plants) are converting sunlight energy to chemical energy in their bodies, but much of this is rapidly being passed on to consumers as the plants are eaten, rather than being stored as living plant material.

3.5 **a** Photosynthesis

b Any from diagram

3.6 **a** At the end of winter, when light intensity, day length and temperatures have all been lower than in summer, so reducing rates of photosynthesis.

b During winter carbon dioxide concentration could rise as more fossil fuels are burnt for heating and electricity generation.

3.7 Where animals graze, their urine and faeces return nitrogen to the soil. When grassland is cut, the nitrogen contained in the grass is removed for hay or silage, and lost to the ccosystem.

Chapter 4

4.1 DNA contains the pentose sugar deoxyribose, while RNA contains ribose.
DNA contains the base thymine, while RNA has uracil.
DNA is made up of two polynucleotide strands, whereas RNA has only one.
DNA molecules are much longer than RNA molecules.

4.2 In polynucleotides, the bases are linked by covalent bonds between phosphate groups and sugars. In NAD, the link is by a covalent bond between two phosphate groups.

4.3 **a** ATP, which phosphorylates the nucleotides, providing energy to drive the reaction.

DNA polymerase, which catalyses the linkage of adjacent nucleotides once they have correctly base-paired.

b The nucleus.

4.4 **a** 64

b For 'punctuation marks', that is for starting or stopping the synthesis of a polypeptide chain. Also, some amino acids could be coded for by two or three different base triplets.

c A two-letter code could only code for 16 amino acids.

4.6 The base T is substituted by the base A.

Chapter 5

5.1 6

5.2 3 homozygous, 3 heterozygous

5.3 **a** Symbols should use the same capital letter, with a different superscript for each allele. For example:

C^R to represent the allele for red coat
C^W to represent the allele for white coat

b $C^R C^R$ red coat
$C^R C^W$ roan coat
$C^W C^W$ white coat

c (i) Red Poll × roan gives $C^R C^R$ (red coat) and $C^R C^W$ (roan coat) in a ratio of 1:1.

(ii) Roan × roan gives $C^R C^R$ (red coat), $C^R C^W$ (roan coat) and $C^W C^W$ (white coat) in a ratio of 1:2:1.

5.4 Symbols should use the same letter of the alphabet, using the capital letter to represent the dominant allele, and the small letter to represent the recessive allele. For example:

B to represent the allele for black eyes
b to represent the allele for red eyes.

The cross would be expected to produce Bb (black eyed mice) and bb (red eyed mice) in a ratio of 1:1.

5.5 If a cross between an unspotted and spotted plant can sometimes produce offspring which are all unspotted, then unspotted must be the dominant allele. Suitable symbols could be:

A to represent the dominant unspotted allele
a to represent the recessive spotted allele

(U and u or S and s are not good choices, as they are difficult to distinguish.)
An unspotted plant could therefore have either the genotype AA or Aa.

A spotted plant could only have the genotype aa.

Therefore, a cross between spotted and unspotted could either be:

Parents   AA × aa
Offspring   Aa

or it could be:

Parents   Aa × aa
Offspring   Aa and aa in a ratio of 1:1.

5.6 She may be right, but not necessarily. It is true that if her bitch were homozygous for the dominant allele for black spots all of her eggs would contain this dominant allele, and therefore all of her offpring would be black no matter what the genotype of the male parent. If the bitch was heterozygous, it might be expected that a mating with a homozygous recessive dog would produce black-spotted and brown-spotted offspring in a ratio of 1:1. However, as only three puppies were born, it may just be chance that no brown-spotted puppy was born. The breeder would need to produce more litters from the bitch before she could be sure of her genotype.

5.7 The child with blood group O must have the genotype I^oI^o. Therefore, each parent must have one I^o allele. The genotypes are therefore :

Man and the child with blood
group B I^BI^o
Woman and the child with blood
group A I^AI^o
Child with blood group O I^oI^o

5.8 Suitable symbols for these four alleles could be :

C^A to represent the agouti allele
C^g to represent the chinchilla (grey) allele
C^h to represent the himalayan allele
C^a to represent the albino allele

a

C^AC^A	agouti
C^AC^g	agouti
C^AC^h	agouti
C^AC^a	agouti
C^gC^g	chinchilla
C^gC^h	chinchilla
C^gC^a	chinchilla
C^hC^h	himalayan
C^hC^a	himalayan
C^aC^a	albino

b (i) The genotype of the albino parent must be C^aC^a, as the allele C^a is recessive to everything else. Each of the offspring will therefore get a C^a allele from this parent. The offspring are all chinchilla, so their genotypes must all be C^gC^a. This means that the chinchilla parent must have given a C^g allele to each offspring, so the chinchilla parent almost certainly has the genotype C^gC^g. If it had any other allele in its genotype, this would be expected to show in the phenotype of its offspring.

When the C^gC^a offspring are crossed, they will produce genotypes of C^gC^g, C^gC^a and C^aC^a in a ratio of 1:2:1, that is a ratio of chinchilla to albino in a ratio of 3:1. This is close enough to the actual ratio of 4 chinchilla to 2 albino, as with these very small numbers it is unlikely for ratios to work out exactly.

(ii) Following similar reasoning to that in (i) above, the agouti rabbit probably has the genotype C^AC^h and the himalayan parent the genotype C^hC^h. This would produce agouti and himalayan offspring in a ratio of 1:1.

(iii) As chinchilla rabbits are produced in the first generation, at least one of the agouti parents must carry a chinchilla allele. As a himalayan rabbit is produced in the second generation, one of the original parents must carry a himalayan allele. The first cross is therefore :

Parents $C^A C^h$ $C^A C^g$

Gametes   (C^A) or (C^h)   (C^A) or (C^g)

Offspring $C^A C^A$ $C^A C^h$ $C^A C^g$ $C^h C^g$

            agouti   agouti   agouti   chinchilla

The second cross, between two chinchilla rabbits with the genotype $C^h C^g$, would be expected to produce offspring with the genotypes $C^h C^h$, $C^h C^g$ and $C^g C^g$ in a ratio of 1:2:1, so giving the phenotypic ratio of 3 chinchilla : 1 himalayan.

5.9   *Parents*   XX   XY

      Gametes   all (X)   (X) or (Y)

      Offspring   XX   or   XY

5.10 a No. The son will receive a Y chromosome from his father, which cannot carry a haemophilia allele.

b Yes. The man could pass on his haemophilia allele to a daughter, who could then pass it on to a son.

5.11 a Suitable symbols could be:

     X^N allele for normal colour vision
     X^n allele for red–green colour blindness
     $X^N X^N$ normal female
     $X^N X^n$ carrier (normal) female
     $X^n X^n$ female with colour blindness
     $X^N Y$ normal male
     $X^n Y$ male with colour blindness

b *Parents' phenotypes*   normal   normal

Parents' genotypes $X^N Y$ $X^N X^n$

Gametes   (X^N) (Y)   (X^N) (X^n)

Offspring genotypes and phenotypes

Genotypes of eggs

	X^N	X^n
X^N	$X^N X^N$ normal female	$X^N X^n$ carrier female
Y	$X^N Y$ normal male	$X^n Y$ male with colour blindness

Genotypes of sperm (left side label)

This can happen if the woman is heterozygous. The affected child will be male.

c Yes, if the mother has at least one allele for colour blindness, and the father has colour blindness.

5.12 a Male cats cannot be tortoiseshell because a tortoiseshell cat has two alleles of this gene. As the gene is on the X chromosome, and male cats have one X chromosome and one Y chromosome, then they can only have one allele of the gene.

b *Parents' phenotypes*   orange male   tortoiseshell female

Parents' genotypes $X^{C^O} Y$ $X^{C^O} X^{C^B}$

Gametes   (X^{C^O}) (Y)   (X^{C^O}) (X^{C^B})

Offspring genotypes and phenotypes

Genotypes of eggs

	X^{C^O}	X^{C^B}
X^{C^O}	$X^{C^O} X^{C^O}$ orange female	$X^{C^O} X^{C^B}$ tortoiseshell female
Y	$X^{C^O} Y$ orange male	$X^{C^B} Y$ black male

Genotypes of sperm (left side label)

The kittens would therefore be expected to be in the ratio of 1 orange female : 1 tortoiseshell female : 1 orange male : 1 black male.

5.13 **a** AaBb and Aabb in a ratio of 1:1

b GgHh, Gghh, gg Hh and gghh in a ratio of 1:1:1:1

c All TtYy

d EeFf, Eeff, eeFf and eeff in a ratio of 1:1:1:1

5.14 **a** They would all have genotype GgTt, and phenotype grey fur and long tail.

b Grey long, grey short, white long, white short in a ratio of 9:3:3:1.

5.15 Let T represent the allele for tall stem, t the allele for short stem, L^G the allele for green leaves and L^W the allele for white leaves.

Parents TTL^GL^G ttL^GL^W

Gametes

Offspring TtL^GL^G, TtL^GL^W in a ratio of 1:1.

5.16 **a** If B represents the allele for black eyes and b represents the allele for red eyes, L represents the allele for long fur and l represents the allele for short fur, then the four possible genotypes of an animal with black eyes and long fur are
BBLL, BbLL, BBLl and BbLl.

b Perform a test cross, that is breed the animal with an animal showing both recessive characteristics. If the offspring show one of the recessive characteristics, then the 'unknown' genotype must be heterozygous for that characteristic.

5.17 Synthesising enzymes which have no use would be a waste of materials (amino acids) and energy.

Chapter 6

6.1 Characteristics are passed from parents to offspring in their genes. Variation caused by the environment does not change the DNA of an organism.

6.2 **a** There seems to be no selection pressure against unusual colours, as there are no predators.

b Possibilities include ability to cope with a limited food or water supply, ability to cope with the limited breeding space, and susceptibility to disease such as myxomatosis if this is present on the island.

6.3 **a** The more frequently antibiotics are used, the more frequently resistant bacteria will be selected for. If antibiotic use is infrequent, then other selection pressures will be more important in bacterial populations, decreasing the likelihood of resistant bacteria surviving.

b Changing the antibiotic changes the selection pressure. Different strains of bacteria will be selected for when a different antibiotic is used, decreasing the likelihood of a resistant strain for each antibiotic becoming widespread.

c It is far less likely that any individual bacterium will be resistant to two antibiotics than to any single antibiotic, so decreasing the chance of any bacteria surviving in an environment where two antibiotics are used together.

Index (Numbers in italics refer to figures.)

Acknowledgements

Photographs

1.13, Andrew Syred 1991 Microscopix; 1.14, Andrew Syred 1989 Microscopix; 1.15, 3.10b, Anton Page; 1.16, 3.10a, 6.9b, 6.12, Biophoto Associates; 2.6 Dr Keith Porter/Science Photo Library; 2.7, Dr J E Walker, MRC Cambridge; 3.12, DR C E Jeffree/Oxford Scientific Films; 3.16, Bob Gibbons/Ardea; 4.10, O L Miller Jr and B A Hamkalo, Visualization of bacterial genes in action, *Science*, **169**, 392–5, 24 July 1970, copyright 1970 by the American Association for the Advancement of Science; 4.11, Omikron/ Science Photo Library; 5.3a, 5.3d, Hans Reinhard/ Bruce Coleman Ltd; 5.3b, Don Hadden/Ardea; 5.3c, John Daniels/Ardea; 5.6, Mr Krzysztof Maj/ Bruce Coleman Ltd; 6.2, Popperfoto; 6.3, Jane Burton/Bruce Coleman Ltd; 6.6, Heather Angel; 6.7, Eric Dragesco/Ardea; 6.8, John Durham/ Science Photo Library; 6.9a, J L Mason/Ardea; 6.13, P Morris/Ardea

Diagrams

3.7, data from Barnola *et al.* 1987 Nature **329**; 408–14; 3.8, from *Climate Change, The UK Programme*, HMSO January 1994; 3.14, from *The nitrogen cycle of the United Kingdom*, 1983, The Royal Society London; 3.15, from *Research on the Nitrogen Cycle – A Sixth Form Study Resource*, Agricultural and Food Research Centre and the National Centre for Biotechnology Education